IKEAHACKERS.NET

25 Biggest and Best Projects

IKEAHACKERS.NET

25 Biggest and Best Projects

DIY Hacks for Multi-Functional Furniture, Clever Storage Upgrades, Space-Saving Solutions and More

Jules Yap
Founder of IkeaHackers.net

Ulysses Press

Published in the United States by:
Ulysses Press
P.O. Box 3440
Berkeley, CA 94703
www.ulyssespress.com

ISBN: 978-1-61243-670-8
Library of Congress Catalog Number 2016957518

Printed in the United States by Bang Printing
10 9 8 7 6 5 4 3 2 1

Acquisitions editor: Casie Vogel
Managing editor: Claire Chun
Editor: Shayna Keyles
Proofreader: Lauren Harrison
Design and layout: what!design @ whatweb.com

Distributed by Publishers Group West

CONTENTS

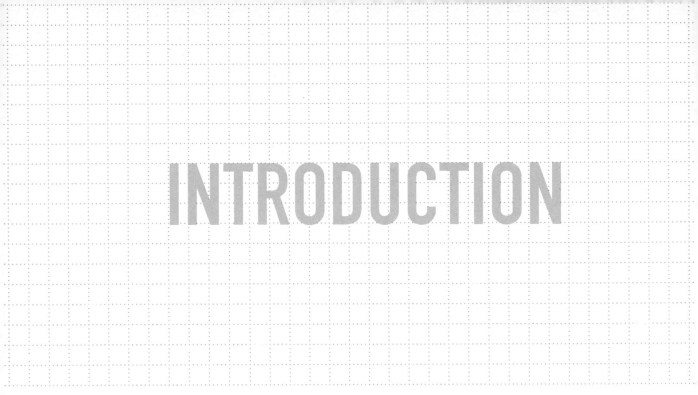

INTRODUCTION

It was June 2006. I was browsing a home decor website looking for ideas to furnish my new apartment. It was then I saw my first IKEA® hack. Up until that moment, I'd always thought of furniture as static—I buy a bed, I get a bed. The article I stumbled across featured a guy who'd bought 2 IKEA® PAX wardrobe sliding doors and made them into a room divider. I didn't know you could do that! I began searching for more hacks, and each find made me more excited than the last. People were doing strange things to IKEA® products, and I loved it!

After a few days, I had collected a handful of hacks from various parts of the World Wide Web. "How wonderful if they could all be housed on one site, for all IKEA® fans to enjoy," I thought to myself. I wasn't sure if anyone else was as crazy about weird IKEA® mods as I was, but with what little blogging skills I had, I started IkeaHackers.net anyway. I updated it as regularly as I could find hacks and didn't think too much about it. As it turned out, a whole lot of people were into hacking, and they started sharing their creations with me. From there, IkeaHackers grew and grew.

Now, you may ask, "What's an IKEA® hack?" In its simplest terms, it's a modification of an IKEA® product. In no way does the term "hack" infer that the mods are sloppily done. Rather, the name suggests that the hackers "break into" the IKEA® "code" of furniture assembly and repurpose, challenge, and create with new results.

People hack IKEA® for many reasons: some to get exactly what they want, some for economic reasons, some for style. Reasons abound. But whatever the reason is, you can be sure it's fun to slice and dice mass-produced flat-pack furniture into something totally different.

This book is to help you do just that.

We've put together some of the biggest and best IKEA® hacks from all over the world. Our hope is that they'll expand your imagination and trigger you to see what's possible with RAST, FROSTA, BILLY and friends. Our sneaky intention is you'll to walk into IKEA® and never see their furniture the same way again. Because it does not have to be.

The book has projects suitable for every level of skill. Some of the projects are easy, while some are tougher to do. Some need nothing more than a drill, while others may require an assortment of tools. Browse through the book and start with projects closer to your ability, then level up as your DIY confidence grows.

As with all DIY projects, safety comes first. In the projects, you may come across steps and tools that you're unsure of. In such instances, please seek help from an expert DIYer. All electrical work should be handled by a professional to ensure compliance to safety regulations. Do check IKEA®'s instructions on the safe use of their products. Please take the precaution to securely anchor all cabinets to the wall. Always make sure that the hacked item is safe for you and those who will use it. Please remind yourself to always err on the side of safety.

Finally, I hope this book inspires you to create IKEA® hacks of your own. There's always something new in IKEA® waiting to be hacked. You could be the one to do so. And I'll be here to share your IKEA® hack with the world.

Happy hacking,

Jules

www.IkeaHackers.net
www.facebook.com/ikeahackers

NOTE: IKEA® product measurements are given in width x depth x height. US lumber measurements are given in height x width x length.

THE PROJECTS

BEAUTIFUL BILLY BESTÅ BEHEMOTH

Tony Tapia and Scott Vedder

Apopka, Florida

This hack combines BESTÅ and BILLY frames in the same project. This is a unique challenge because the heights and depths of both collections are different. Matching them up requires cutting the BILLY frames to the right height and then boosting the BESTÅs to match. No worries, though! This project can be completed by anyone with a sense of adventure, a little know-how around a few power tools, and plenty of time and patience. At the end, Tony and Scott wound up with a custom piece that looks professionally built but cost less than $1,400.

When this hack was assembled, VASSBO doors were offered. If available, use 14 assorted BESTÅ VASSBO doors. However, VASSBO is unavailable in most markets, but SINDVIK is the most similar style of door currently found at IKEA® locations.

IKEA® Home Furnishings

- 2 BESTÅ frames, 23⅝×15¾×75⅝ inches (60×40×192 cm)
- 3 double BESTÅ frames, 23⅝×15¾×25¼ inches (60×40×64 cm)
- 3 single BESTÅ cabinets, 23⅝×15¾×15 inches (60×40×38 cm)
- 2 BILLY bookcases, 15¾×11×79½ inches (40×28×202 cm)
- 16 assorted SINDVIK doors and drawer fronts, to fit
- OXBERG panel doors to fit BESTÅ frames, 15¾×75⅝ inches (40×192 cm)
- BESTÅ rails
- two 4-piece DIODER light strip sets (optional)

Materials

- 10 2×4-inch (5×10¼-cm) boards, 96 inches (243¾ cm) long
- electric circular saw, blade diameter at least 6½ inches (16½ cm)
- 1½-inch (38-mm) wide-thread multipurpose screws
- wood glue
- painter's tape (optional)
- builder's caulk
- hammer
- nail gun (optional)

- 1-inch (2½-cm) furring strips, 24 feet (7¼ meters)
- drill

- 2-inch (51-mm) rotary bit
- baseboard trim
- crown molding

Instructions

1. Build all of the BILLY and BESTÅ frames according to the assembly instructions.

2. Make a rectangle base for each of your 75⅝-inch-wide BESTÅ frames using the 2×4s. Measure the bottom of the BESTÅ to determine the dimensions of the rectangular base; it should match the dimensions of the base of the BESTÅ exactly. Each base should consist of four boards, cut to size using a circular saw, then screwed together at the corners at right angles. Attach the bases to the bottom of the BESTÅ units with wood glue.

3. Lay the first BESTÅ on its right side and then place a BILLY horizontally on top of the BESTÅ. Align the tops and faces of the cabinets so they are flush. Temporarily attach the frames together using the inter-cabinet connector screws included with the BESTÅ. You can also use painter's tape to hold them together.

4. You'll notice that the foot of the BILLY extends about ¾ inch past the adjoining BESTÅ and its rectangular base. Make a mark on the BILLY indicating where the bottom of the BESTÅ base ends, and then use the circular saw to cut the BILLY frame to the marked length.

5. Attach the BILLY and BESTÅ together using glue and screws as needed. Align the bases of both pieces so that the towers stand level when

finally assembled. The completed piece will be one of the side towers.

6. Repeat Steps 3 through 5 to create the second side tower, but lay the BESTÅ on its left side rather than its right side to ensure symmetrical towers. At the end of this step, you should have two sets of BILLY/BESTÅ side towers for the outer ends of the installation.

7. To assemble the central pedestal, attach three double BESTÅ cabinets together using the screws included in the BESTÅ packaging. You can add builder's caulk between the cabinets for added strength.

8. Create a wooden base for the central pedestal to match the bases on the side towers. This will also raise the pedestal off the floor, allow room for the doors, and make it easier to attach baseboard trim later. Create and attach a rectangular base to the central pedestal using the same technique as described in Step 2. This should require no more than three of your 96-inch 2×4s. Attach the bases with glue. Keep the central pedestal and side towers separate.

9. To create the suspended bridge portion of the design, attach the remaining three BESTÅ units

to the wall using the IKEA® BESTÅ rails, following the assembly instructions.

10. After the bridge is anchored safely on the wall, combine the other completed units into a single built-in. Center the pedestal underneath the bridge, then align the side towers so they are symmetrical and snug against the center pedestal and the bridge. Screw and glue each unit to the next.

11. Add baseboard trim and crown molding to the unit to match the rest of the house and to cover the bases of each unit. Use the measurements of the installation as a guide for cutting the molding. Miter the baseboard and molding corners using a circular saw. Attach the baseboard trim, using a nail gun if available, to the rectangular bases and along the front of the bottoms of the BILLY cabinets using a nail gun. Attach 1-inch furring strips to the top of the installation, then attach the crown molding on top of that.

12. Attach doors that correspond to the BESTÅ unit sizes and match your design vision and needs. The doors are attached to the BESTÅ frames by using the hinges included in the IKEA® packaging.

13. Optionally, attach DIODER light strips in any glass compartments. Place the LED strips on the inside of the door near the hinges, using the adhesive included in the IKEA® packaging. To hide the cables, drill a ½-inch hole in the top of each frame where the lights are being installed and run the cables through. Hide all of the cables and switches behind the cabinet. The switches can be installed inside the left BILLY frame using a 2-inch circular drill bit to open a 2-inch circular hole in the back wall of the BILLY. You can then pass the switches and wires through the hole. The switches will be accessible, while the cables are neatly stashed away out of sight behind the unit.

About the Contributors

Tony Tapia and Scott Vedder hack because they often can't find store-bought solutions that match their style and suit the exact dimensions and scale of their home. They also don't want to hire a designer, engineer, and architect every time a new cabinet is needed. But mostly, they hack because they enjoy working together on projects. When family and friends visit, they often exclaim, "Wow, where did you get that piece?" Tony and Scott feel an enormous sense of pride and accomplishment when they reply, "We built it!" They hope that their hack inspires others as much as the hacks they've found online have inspired them. The two are married and live in Apopka, Florida. They share a single-family house with their four shar-pei dogs, Maya, Lenox, Castor, and Pollux.

MODERNIST TEA TROLLEY

Danielle Connelly

New York, New York

For this project, Danielle referenced a piece of modern design by Alvar Aalto. By redefining the intended purpose of two FROSTA stools, she was able to create Aalto's Tea Trolley 901 from the 1930s. The design of the cart was an adaptation of the language and techniques developed for Aalto's three-legged stool, one of the most well-known designs of modern times. Danielle has repurposed all parts of the globally ubiquitous FROSTA stool, including the hardware, to create this cleverly constructed and easily replicated hack of the seminal Aalto Tea Trolley.

IKEA® Home Furnishings

- 2 FROSTA stools

Materials

- tape measure
- carpenter's square
- pencil
- 2 clamps
- handsaw
- drill
- 1-inch (25-mm) Forstner bit
- standard drill bit set
- masking tape (optional)
- 180-grit sandpaper
- wood glue
- 16 wood screws, ¾ inch (19 mm) long

- wood filler
- 2 birch veneer cabinetry-grade plywood sheets, FSC certified and formaldehyde-free, 16×¾×29 inches (40¾×2×73¾ cm)
- 2 wooden dowels, $3/_8$ inch (1 cm) long
- rubber mallet
- damp cloth
- 2 PVC pipe routing clamps, 1¼ inches ($3^1/_8$ cm)
- 1 PVC pipe, 1×16 inches ($2^1/_2$×$40^5/_8$ cm)
- 1 wooden dowel, 1×33 inches ($2^1/_2$×84 cm) long
- $2^3/_8$×2-inch (1×5-cm) wooden dowels
- Two ¼×1½-inch ($5/_8$×$3^3/_4$-cm) wooden dowels

Instructions

1. Open one FROSTA stool and set the top aside. On each of the legs, measure 9 inches from the end opposite the predrilled holes. Square off with a pencil. Clamp down to the workbench and use the handsaw to cut 9 inches off each of the legs. Retain the curved portion of each leg, labeling two as "A" and two as "B." Set the straight 9-inch pieces aside as scrap wood.

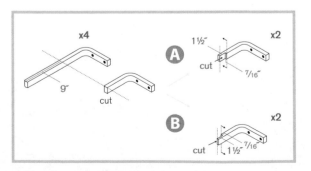

2. For both "A" pieces, measure 1½ inches up from the cut end and square off. Then, measure $7/_{16}$ inch from the inside of the leg to divide the side of the leg in half. Mark this portion of leg "A" with a pencil, then clamp the leg pieces down for stability. With the longer end of the leg pointing up, use your handsaw to carefully remove the 1½×$7/_{16}$-inch portion from the inside of the leg. Repeat for the other leg. It's always better to cut less and sand down later than to cut too much; for all of your cuts, err toward cutting on the offcut side of the line.

3. For both "B" pieces, measure 1½ inches up from the cut end and square off. Then, measure $7/_{16}$ inch from the outside of the leg to divide the side of the leg in half. Mark this portion of leg "B" with a pencil; the offcut on piece "B" should align with the offcut on piece "A." Clamp the leg pieces down for stability. With the longer end of the leg pointing up, use your handsaw to carefully remove the 1½×⁷/₁₆-inch portion from the outside of the leg. Repeat for the other leg.

4. Open the second FROSTA stool and set the top aside. Label two legs "C" and two legs "D." For both legs labeled "C," measure 2½ inches up the middle of the side of the leg, from the end opposite the predrilled holes, and square off with a pencil. Clamp down for stability, and using a handsaw, cut 2½ inches off the two legs.

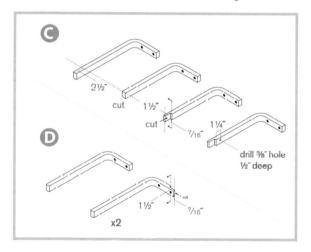

5. Measure 1½ inches up from the cut end of the "C" legs, then measure ⁷/₁₆ inch from the inside of the leg to divide the side of the leg in half. Mark this portion of leg "C" with a pencil. Clamp the piece for stability, with the longer end pointing up, and carefully remove the 1½×⁷/₁₆-inch portion from the inside of the leg. Repeat for second piece.

6. While the "C" legs are still clamped to the table, measure 1¼ inch up from the offcut on the inside of the leg. Drill a ³/₈-inch hole, ½ inch deep, in the center of the inside of each leg. To be sure not to drill through your leg, measure ½ inch up your drill bit and add a piece of tape for reference. You will only drill to the point that the wood touches the masking tape, which will prevent you from drilling all the way through the wood.

7. For both "D" legs, measure 1½ inches in from the end with the predrilled holes. Square off, then measure ⁷/₁₆ inch from the outside of the leg to divide the side of the leg in half. Mark this portion of leg "D" with a pencil. Clamp the piece for stability, with the shorter end pointing up, and carefully remove the 1½×⁷/₁₆-inch portion from the outside of the leg. Repeat for second piece.

8. Overlap one "A" piece with one "B" piece to create a curved leg. If necessary, wrap sand paper around a leg offcut to sand and refine the joint. When satisfied with the joint fit, add an even but generous layer of wood glue to the joining surfaces of "A" and "B." Clamp the newly formed leg "AB" to the table, with the end with predrilled holes sticking up vertically. Use a ¹/₁₆-inch bit to drill 3 new ¾-inch deep pilot holes through the joint, and screw in 3 wood screws from "B" to "A" to secure the lap joint. (To be sure not to drill through the leg, measure ¾ inch up your drill bit and add a piece of tape for reference.) If there are gaps in the joint, fill with several thin layers of wood filler. Wipe with a damp rag to remove excess, then let layers dry in between. Repeat for the remaining "A" and "B" pieces to create a matching curved leg.

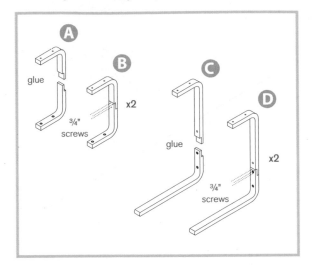

appearance of the veneer, place the "better" side facedown for the following steps.

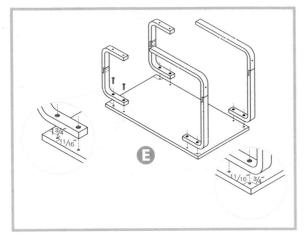

9. Overlap one "C" piece with one "D" piece to create a curved leg with one long end. If necessary, wrap sand paper around a leg offcut to sand and refine the joint. Then, add an even but generous layer of wood glue to the joining surfaces of "C" and "D." Clamp the newly formed leg "CD" to the table with the predrilled holes sticking up vertically. Use a $^1/_{16}$-inch bit to drill 3 new ¾-inch deep pilot holes through the joint, and screw in 3 wood screws to secure the lap joint from "D" to "C." (To be sure not to drill through your leg, measure ¾ inch up your drill bit and add a piece of tape for reference). If there are gaps in the joint, fill with several thin layers of wood filler. Wipe with a damp rag to remove excess, then let layers dry in between. Repeat for the two remaining "C" and "D" pieces to create a matching curved leg.

10. Label one plywood shelf "E" and the other "F." If you are concerned with the cosmetic

11. Starting with shelf "E" in front of you length-wise, measure 1¾ inches in from the left edge and draw a vertical line across the entire shelf. On the right edge, measure ¾ inch in, then draw another vertical line across the entire shelf. Next, measure $^{11}/_{16}$ inch in from the front and back edges, and draw lines horizontally from these points. At the intersections of the four lines, use a $^3/_{16}$-inch bit to drill pilot holes ½ inch deep. Be careful not to drill all the way through the plywood.

12. Take both "AB" legs and line up the predrilled holes that are closer to the curve of the leg with the pilot holes you just drilled on the left side of shelf "E." Make sure the vertical part of the curve is on the left. Clamp the legs to "E," avoiding the holes. With two of the screws and the Allen wrench that came with the FROSTA stools, secure the legs to "E" by screwing down through the leg's outer predrilled hole and into the shelf's pilot hole. Once the "AB" legs are tacked in place, use the empty predrilled hole as a template to drill subsequent pilot holes, then finish securing the "AB" legs with FROSTA screws.

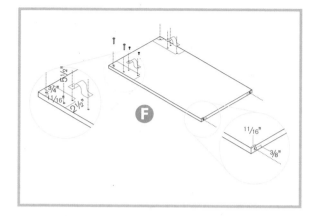

13. Take both "CD" legs and line up the predrilled holes on the short end of the curve, with the pilot holes you drilled earlier on the right side of "E." Clamp legs to "E," avoiding the predrilled holes. With two of the screws and the Allen wrench that came with the FROSTA stools, secure the legs to "E" by screwing down through the right predrilled hole of the leg and into the pilot hole in the shelf. Once the "CD" legs are tacked in place, use the empty predrilled hole as a template to drill subsequent pilot holes, then finish securing the "CD" legs with FROSTA screws.

14. Lay "F" lengthwise in front of you. On the right edge of the board, measure $^{11}/_{16}$ inch in from the front and back sides, then use a $^{3}/_{8}$-inch bit to drill a 1½-inch deep pilot hole into the middle of the board's edge. You may want to stand the shelf up vertically so it's easier to drill into edge of the board. Next, measure ¾ inch in from the left edge and draw a vertical line across the board. Then, measure $^{11}/_{16}$ inch in from the front and back

edges. Use your square to trace two horizontal lines across the board. At the intersections of the three lines, use a $^{3}/_{16}$-inch bit to drill pilot holes ½ inch deep. Do not drill through the plywood; use tape on your drill bit as a reference, if needed.

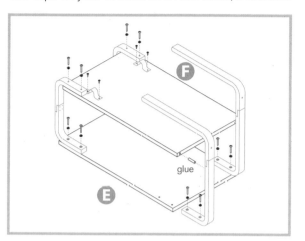

15. Clamp "F" to the underside of the unattached curved end of "AB" legs, making sure to align the predrilled holes in the legs with the pilot holes you just drilled in "F." You will need to prop up the right side of "F" in order to keep it level. With two of the screws and the Allen wrench that came with the FROSTA stools, secure the "AB" legs to "F" by screwing down through the left predrilled hole of the leg and into the pilot hole in the bottom of the shelf. Once "F" is tacked in place, use the empty predrilled holes of "AB" leg as a template to drill subsequent pilot holes. Finish securing "F" with FROSTA screws.

16. Once the pilot holes on the right edge of "F" are aligned with the pilot holes drilled on the "CD" legs, cover your two $^{3}/_{8}$-inch wooden dowels with wood glue and insert one end into "F" and the other into "CD" leg to complete the dowel joint.

Tap with rubber mallet to seal and wipe away any excess glue with a damp rag.

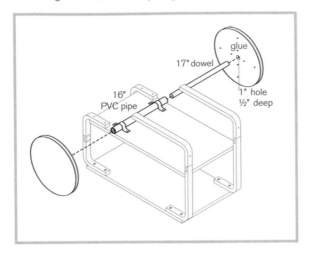

17. To finish "F," attach the pipe clamps that will hold the PVC pipe axle. Measure 5½ inches in from the left edge of "F" and draw a vertical line across the board. Then measure 2½ inches in from the front and back edges and draw horizontal lines across the board. Where these lines intersect, use a $1/16$-inch bit to drill pilot holes ½ inch deep. Align the predrilled holes on the left sides of the pipe clamps with the new pilot hole, and screw into place. Make sure the clamps are parallel with the front and back edges of "F," then drill pilot holes and screw down the right-hand side of the clamp.

18. To make the wheels and axle, start by using the predrilled holes on the underside of the FROSTA seat to find the center of the circle. Using your 1-inch Forstner bit, drill a ½-inch deep hole directly on your center mark, making sure to keep the drill perpendicular to the seat. Repeat for second wheel.

19. Using some leg offcuts clamped to the table, create a vice in which to clamp your PVC pipe down. Measure, mark, and cut the pipe to a 16-inch length.

20. Using the same vice system, clamp your 33-inch long wooden dowel and cut it into one 17-inch piece for the axle and one 16-inch piece for the handle.

21. While the 16-inch piece of wooden dowel is clamped in the vice, draw a straight line along the length of the dowel. Now, measure $11/16$ inch in from each end, and mark. On the marks, use a ¼-inch bit to drill a pilot hole ¾ inch deep into the wooden rod.

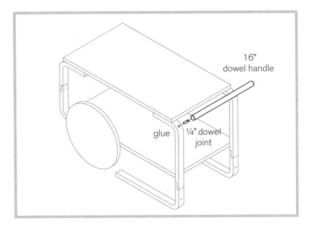

22. To assemble the wheel axle, slide the PVC pipe under the pipe clamps attached to "F." Then, slide the 17-inch wooden dowel through the PVC pipe so that it sticks out ½ inch on either end. It will friction-fit into the 1-inch holes drilled into the wheels; you may need to sand the ends of your dowel to fit it into the holes. Apply an even layer of glue and insert the dowel into the wheels. Tap with a rubber mallet to seal, and wipe away any excess glue with a damp rag.

23. Flip the entire piece over in order to attach the handle. The handle is joined to the cart with a dowel joint into "CD" legs; tape along the edge of the top shelf as a guide to help you position the dowel holes approximately 1 inch away from the shelf. Find the center of each leg and use a ¼-inch bit to drill a pilot hole ¾ inch deep at a 45-degree angle into the curve of the leg. Make sure the holes are in alignment, or your dowel joint won't fit. Trim the ¼-inch dowel down to a 1½-inch length. Test the alignment of your dowel joint between the legs and the handle. When satisfied, cover the dowels in an even layer of glue and insert one end into the leg and one end into the handle. Tap with a rubber mallet to seal, and wipe away any excess glue with a damp rag.

24. Fill any unwanted holes with thin layers of wood filler, and enjoy!

About the Contributor

Danielle Connelly is part of the Industrial Design MFA program at Parsons, The New School, and holds a degree in Architecture from Princeton University. After nearly five years of practicing architecture in Shanghai, China, Danielle relocated to New York to further explore her capabilities as a product designer. Her professional endeavors and personal growth in Asia have afforded her great skills in blending space and craft, along with an acute sense for detail and a compulsive drive to explore our daily relationships with the objects around us.

HEXAGON SHELVING UNIT

Jules Yap and Martin Wong

Malaysia

This stackable shelving unit looks great against a wall or as a room divider. Plus, you can change the formation whenever you want to!

IKEA® Home Furnishings

- 2 RAST nightstands per single hexagon unit

Materials

- circular saw
- measuring tape
- drill
- 2-mm and 4½-mm drill bits
- 1½-inch (38-mm) screws
- wood filler
- fine and coarse sandpaper

- cloth or rag
- primer
- paint
- foam paint roller
- paintbrush
- metal dowels
- Phillips screwdriver

Instructions

1. Unpack two sets of RAST nightstands. You should end up with 4 long boards ("A," "B," "E," and "F") and 4 short boards ("C," "D," "G," and "H").

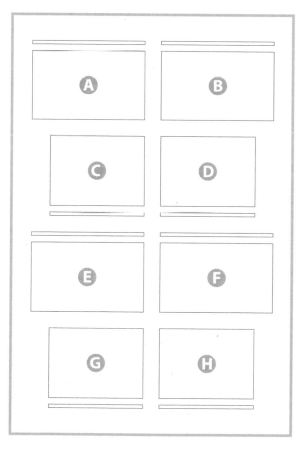

2. Adjust your circular saw to cut off 30 degrees.

3. Cut "A" and "E" to 16¾ inches (42.5 cm) with a 30-degree cut on each end.

4. Trim the other six boards to a length of 11¾ inches (29.6 cm), with a 30-degree cut on each end.

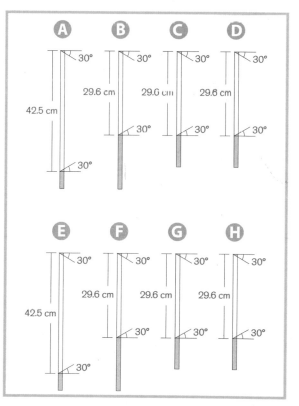

5. Optional step: The short boards and long boards have a slight difference in width. You can trim the boards to equal widths so that your hexagon units will look neater. If not, it's okay too. Just remember to keep the face of the unit flush when screwing the unit together so the variance will be at the back of the unit.

6. Gather "B," "C," "D," "F," "G," and "H," and align the bevel cuts to create your hexagon shape. Drill pilot holes using the 2-mm drill bits and screw the boards together. Two screws on each side should do it. Countersink the screws if you plan to cover up the screw heads.

7. Slide "A" and "E" into the hollow of the hexagon. The bevel edges should sit flush against the sides of the hexagon. Screw the shelves to the sides of the hexagon.

8. Fill all countersunk holes with wood filler and let dry.

9. Sand the boards, first with the coarse grit sandpaper, then with the fine grit. Wipe down the boards with a dry rag to remove all debris.

10. Use the foam roller to apply primer on the outside of the hexagon. Carefully brush primer on the edges with the paintbrush. Let it dry and then lightly go over the primed sections with fine sandpaper again to remove any build up.

11. Use the foam roller to apply paint of your choice to the sides of the hexagon, again using a paintbrush for the edges. We left the inside of the hexagon natural for a nice contrast.

12. Repeat instructions 1 through 11 to make a few more units.

13. To join the units together, drill 4 dowel holes into the sides with the 4½-mm drill bit. Check that the diameter of the dowel corresponds with the size of the drill bit before drilling. You will need four dowels for each board that will attach to another unit, one dowel for each corner. Each dowel hole should be located 1¼×⅞ inches (3×2 cm) from a corner. Pop in the dowels and insert another shelving unit on top of them, aligning dowels to holes.

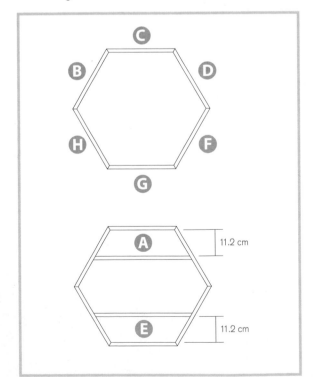

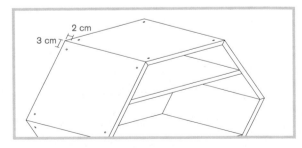

Notes from the Contributors

Jules and Martin used dowels to join the units because they wanted the flexibility of shape shifting. However, if you have young kids at home or want to place heavy or expensive items on this shelving unit, you should join them together with screws, which are much more secure. If using as a room divider, you may want to also secure the units together with screws, as well as bracket one end to a wall.

KITCHEN ISLAND

Sofia Clara
Switzerland

Sofia's new apartment has a fairly big kitchen, leaving plenty of space for a kitchen island, but she couldn't afford to spend extra on one. She had an IKEA® FINNVARD desk, and after a little brainstorming, she figured that the legs could be used as a starting point for a kitchen island. "The great thing about FINNVARD desk legs is that you can mount them at different heights, meaning we could have a work top high enough, as well as shelving space underneath It now serves as extra worktop space, extra storage space, and a high breakfast table," she says.

IKEA® Home Furnishings

- **2 FINNVARD trestle legs**

Materials

- 1 wooden board, 47¼×31½ inches (120×80 cm)
- 2 wooden boards, 35½×13¾ inches (90×35 cm)
- fine sandpaper
- food-safe kitchen worktop wood protection rub
- rasp or jigsaw
- masking tape
- cloth
- pencil
- drill
- 6-mm drill bit
- 1½-inch (38-mm) long screws with head no greater than ¼-inch (8-mm) diameter

Instructions

1. Start by mounting the FINNVARD desk legs, following the assembly instructions.

2. Sand the wooden boards with fine sandpaper to make sure they are smooth, then follow the instructions to rub the kitchen worktop protection onto the wooden boards using your cloth.

3. Once dry, carefully mark on the 35½-inch boards to indicate where cuts will be made for the removable top part of the FINNVARD desk legs. You will need to cut rectangles measuring $2^{1}/_{8} \times {}^{7}/_{8}$ inches to fit the legs; measure the legs to double check the size. Placing the two boards together to form a single, 35½×27½-inch slab, mark the areas for your cuts 1½ inches from the edges of the short side of the board and 2 inches from the edge of the long side of the board. You should have four total rectangles.

4. Using a drill, drill 14 holes inside each of the areas you marked out and then use a rasp to file down the area to get a clean rectangle. If you have a jigsaw, you could just drill one hole and use the jigsaw to cut out the rectangle and sand down with sandpaper or a rasp.

5. Once you have checked that the rectangles are the right size, you can piece your unit together. Start by spacing the two FINNVARD leg bases 35½ inches apart. Place the two 35½-inch boards on top of the desk legs. The edges of the boards should be aligned with the edges of the top of the desk legs. This now forms your middle shelf.

6. Push the top, removable parts of the trestles through the rectangles you cut in the middle shelf.

7. Use the wooden pegs provided with the desk legs to lock them at the right height. Then place the larger wooden board on top. To secure the large board of wood on top, turn it upside down and screw one of the screws 7¾ inches from the shorter edge of the board and 3¼ inches from the longer edge of the work top. You will need to do this twice on diagonal corners. The screws should be on the unvarnished side of the worktop and will fit into existing holes on the top of the FINNVARD legs to hold the work top on securely.

8. Fill up with kitchen goodies.

About the Contributor

Sofia Clara is a Swiss lifestyle blogger over at sofiaclara.com where she shares a happy, homemade way of life. From recipes to DIY décor and fashion ideas, she encourages people to get creative and start making, baking, and building a space, a home, and a life they love. Connect with Sofia at www.sofiaclara.com

HALF-WALL LAMP

Jules Yap and Martin Wong

Malaysia

Jules and Martin had the crazy idea to turn a single FROSTA stool into a wall lamp, but they were stuck on how to make the shade. They were looking for something to hold up the rings for the shade when Martin exclaimed, "Allen wrenches!" And thanks to IKEA®, they had an abundance of those. It turned out to be a great fit for the lamp and reduced their stockpile considerably.

IKEA® Home Furnishings

- FROSTA stool

Materials

- pencil
- jigsaw
- compass
- drill
- masking tape
- measuring tape
- Phillips screwdriver
- 15 L-shaped Allen wrenches

- 1¼-inch (32-mm) screws
- ¾-inch (19-mm) screws
- lamp socket
- electrical cord
- staple gun and staples
- router
- grinder (if needed)
- bulb

To make the shade:

1. Unpack, but do not assemble, the FROSTA stool. You should have one round seat and four identical legs.

2. Flip the seat over and draw a line through the middle, dividing it into equal halves. Use a jigsaw to cut the seat into two. Label one half "A."

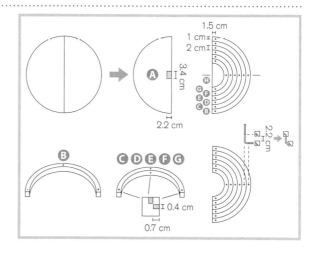

3. On the center of the long side of "A," cut a 1³/₈×⁷/₈-inch (3.5×2.2-cm) notch with a jigsaw. This notch will later hug the FROSTA leg. Set aside.

4. On the other half of the seat, use a compass to draw 6 semicircles, starting from the outer ring toward the center, leaving a ¾-inch (2-cm) gap between each line. Cut along the lines with a jigsaw. At the end, you should have 6 semicircles, each approximately ¾ inch (2 cm) wide. From longest to shortest, label these pieces "B" (13¾ inches, 35 cm), "C" (12¼ inches, 31 cm), "D" (10⁵/₈ inches, 23 cm), "E" (9 inches), "F" (7½ inches, 19 cm), and "G" (6 inches, 15.2 cm). The core, which should be labeled H, should have a diameter of about 4½ inches (11.5 cm).

5. Choose a drill bit that is one size larger in diameter than your Allen wrenches (our Allen wrenches were 3 mm, so we used a 4-mm drill bit). Prepare your drill bit by covering the top of the bit with masking tape so that only ¼ inch (.6 cm) of the tip of your drill bit is exposed. You will only drill to the point that the wood touches the masking tape, which will prevent you from drilling all the way through the wood.

6. On the bottoms of each semicircle, drill one hole on each end, ¾×½ inches (1.5×1 cm) from the edge; then, drill another hole in the center of the semicircle. On the bottom face of each semicircle, you should end up with 3 holes. The holes should be ¹/₈ inch wide and ¼ inch deep (.4×.7 cm). You may need to adjust the size of these holes accordingly to fit the Allen wrenches you have.

7. Drill another three holes on each semicircle, now on the inside edge, as pictured in the bottom center image in the diagram on page 25. The positions and sizes of these holes should correspond to the holes drilled in Step 6. When all the holes are drilled on the semicircles, set them aside for later.

8. Take 2 FROSTA legs and label them "J" and "K." At the top of the long side of each leg, cut a notch measuring ⁷/₈×1½ inches (2.2×3.5 cm). The notch for "J" should be on the right and for "K," it should be on the left. Set these aside.

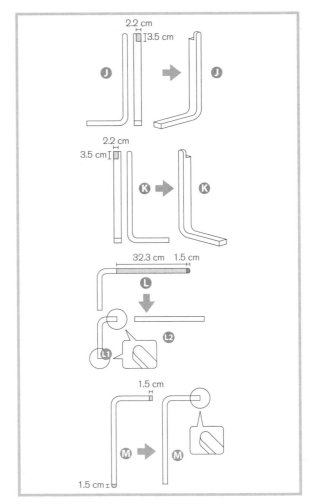

9. Take the third leg and label it "L." Cut it with a jigsaw at 12¾ inches (32.3 cm), giving you two pieces, "L1" and "L2." Remove the rounded tip on "L2," leaving a flat edge. Round both ends of the smaller piece, "L1," with a jigsaw. Set aside both pieces.

10. Label the remaining leg "M." From the long end, cut about ⅝ inch (1.5 cm) off the tip to create a flat bottom. On the shorter end, round the edges with a jigsaw.

To assemble the lamp:

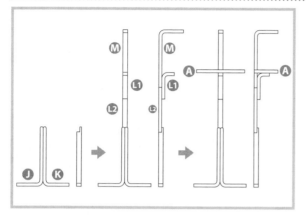

11. Place "J" and "K" with the long ends back to back. The notched portions of the legs should align. Screw them together from "J" to "K," about 4 inches above the base.

12. Sit "L2" in the notch formed by "J" and "K." Use a screwdriver to attach "L2" into the notch. Be careful not to pierce through to the front of "J" and "K."

13. Align the top end of "L2" and the bottom end of "M" together, then place "L1" on top of both pieces, centralizing the joint to the center of "L1." Use the original FROSTA screws and predrilled holes on "L1" to attach it to "L2" and "M." We also added 2 more screws, equally spaced out between the predrilled holes, for added security.

14. Attach "A" to "L1," screwing them together from the underside of "L1" into "A" and also from "M" into "A." This serves as your tray table.

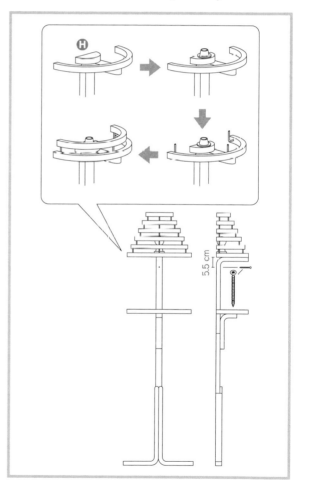

15. "H" will act as the base of your lampshade. Before you attach it to "M," drill the right-sized hole (ours was ³/₈ inch) for your electrical wire. Then attach "H" to the neck of "M," screwing from "H" into "M," making sure that the backs of both pieces are flush.

16. Use a router to rout a channel at the back of the stand for the electrical cord to go through. Attach the socket at "H." To keep the wire in place in the routed channel, fire staples with a staple gun across the routed channel along the back of the stand. Leave a gap of 6 inches between staples.

17. To assemble the shade, screw in the first semicircle "B" to the outer tip of "M."

18. Push the short end of an Allen wrench into one of the holes in the inner edge of semicircle "B." Continue until all 3 holes on the cross section of "B" have an Allen wrench. The longer end of the wrench should point upward. Now take semicircle "C," align the long ends of the wrenches from "B" against the holes on the underside of "C," and push the semicircle down. Then, insert wrenches into the cross section holes of "C," with the long side pointing up. Stack semicircle "D" on top of "C." Repeat this process until all semicircles are attached.

19. When assembled, the gap between each ring should be approximately 1 inch (2.2 cm). If the Allen wrenches you have are too long or of various lengths, shorten them with a grinder. The

Allen wrenches used for this project measure approximately 1½ inches (4 cm) on the long end, ¾ inch (2 cm) on the short end, and ¹/₈ inch (3 mm) in diameter.

20. To attach to the wall, we drilled a hole for a wall screw 2¼ inches (5.5 cm) from the neck of the shade. Hang up with hardware suitable for your wall. As the legs support the stand on the floor, one screw was all it needed to hold the lamp flat against the wall.

21. Screw in the bulb and voilà! A wall lamp so slim, it hardly takes up any real estate.

SWEET STOLMEN WINDOW SEAT

Gretchen Howard

Washington, United States

Gretchen had a problem. Her living room was long and narrow, which made it hard to furnish. For six years, she tried to figure out some way to put seating there, but it always felt too far away from the rest of the furnishing. On top of that, there was limited storage in the space, and her boys' toys, LEGOs, and games were taking over the area.

"I looked at all of the low drawers in the IKEA® catalog, considering their size and style. With luck, I found both of the low STOLMEN drawer sets in the As-Is section of our IKEA®, and the wooden top was there too, in exactly the right size! Later, I added in the two smaller sets in the corner to add balance and more storage to the area."

Some hacking later, she had her customized, built-in window seat for less than $500! The moral of the story? Always check out As-Is before hacking.

If the STOLMEN units are not available in your location, you can use two NORDLI four-drawer-wide dressers and one BRIMNES four-drawer-tall dresser instead.

IKEA® Home Furnishings

- 2 STOLMEN drawers, 43¼×19¾×17¾ inches (102½×50×45 cm)
- 2 narrow STOLMEN drawers, 21⅝×19¾×17¾ inches (55×50×45 cm)
- EKBACKEN countertop

Materials

- measuring tape
- eight 2×4-inch (5×10¼-cm) boards, 23¼ inches (60 cm) long
- six 2×4-inch (5×10¼-cm) boards, 20¼ inches (51½ cm) long
- drill
- screws
- L-brackets
- circular saw
- wood filler

Instructions

1. Remove the baseboard trim from the wall, if any. Set aside.

2. Unpack the STOLMEN units. Find the bottom and back panels of both of the wide units and of one of the narrow units.

3. Orient the bottom panel of the narrow STOLMEN unit so that the long edge faces you, with the finished side of the panel facing up. Measure and mark 1½ inches from each side; this is so you can leave a gap between the edge of the panel and the 2×4s. Trim 2×4s as needed using the circular saw. Align two of the 20¼-inch 2×4s flush with inside of the markings and the top edge of the panel that is facing you. The boards will extend 3½ inches past the opposite edge. Drill through the 2×4 to screw into the panel.

4. Orient the back panel of the narrow STOLMEN unit so that the 21⅝-inch side faces you, with the finished side of the panel facing up. Stand two of the 23¼-inch 2×4s on their narrow edges, with one flush against the left side of the panel and one flush against the right side. They will leave a 3½-inch overhang on one edge of the panel. Drill through the 2×4s to screw into the panel.

5. Repeat Steps 3 and 4 to attach 2×4s to the back and bottom panels of the wide STOLMEN units.

6. On the bottom panels of the wide STOLMEN units, attach an additional 23¼-inch 2×4 centered between the existing 2×4s, using the method described in Step 4. You should wind up with three 2×4s extending 3½ inches beyond the panel.

7. Assemble STOLMEN units according to IKEA® directions. Do not insert drawers. Be careful when aligning 2×4s; you want them to form right-angle joints where they meet. Secure these joints using L-brackets.

8. Place the STOLMEN units against the wall, with the narrow unit in a corner and the two wide units next to it. Align STOLMEN units so that the 2×4 joints are flush against the wall and the units are flush against each other. Use L-brackets to secure the 2×4s to the wall.

9. Place the assembled narrow STOLMEN unit without 2×4s on top of the other narrow unit. Secure by screwing through the base of the top unit into the top of the bottom unit.

10. Set EKBACKEN on top of the wide STOLMEN units and adjust so it is flush with the wall and the narrow STOLMEN unit. Secure the ECKBACKEN top from inside the STOLMEN units with a countersink drill bit, then fill in with wood filler.

11. Insert drawers into the STOLMEN units. Reattach baseboard trim, and you're done!

About the Contributor

As a fifth grade teacher, Gretchen encourages her students to take risks and look for ways to solve their own problems. With that in mind, she tries to live by example, and hacking is a way to do that. For years, Gretchen worked and lived on sailboats, so she's always trying to figure out how to use space efficiently. But between teaching and parenting, she doesn't have the time to build many things from scratch. IKEA® hacks allow her to meet that need.

She lives in a house in Bellingham, Washington, with her husband, two boys, five chickens, and a cat.

CUSTOM SPOTLIGHT VANITY

Jules Yap and Martin Wong

Malaysia

The 3-drawer RAST chest had all the right materials for a dressing table and vanity. It includes one regular drawer, while the other two drawers were hacked to form pullout cabinets behind a mirrored top. It was perfect! The only hard part was figuring out how to lengthen the sides and create a homemade mirrored box top. But once that was hacked, the rest was easy.

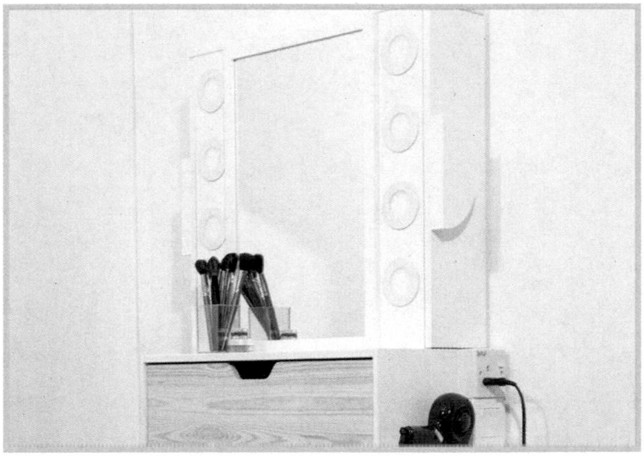

IKEA® Home Furnishings

- **RAST chest of 3 drawers**

- **1 pair TOSTERUP handles**

Materials

- 2 plywood sheets, 11¾×½×30 inches (30×1¼×76½ cm)

- 1 plywood sheet, 3⅝×½×11¾ inches (7½×1½×30 cm)

- drill

- hole saw, 2-inch (51-mm) diameter

- 1¼-inch (32-mm) screws

- 2-inch (51-mm) screws

- jigsaw

- 2 plywood sheets, 23×½×23⅛ inches (58¼×1¼×58¾ cm)

- 1 plywood sheet, 5¼×½×23 inches (58¼×1¼×13¼ cm)

- 2 plywood sheets, 1½×½×13¾ inches (4×1¼×35 cm)

- 8 LED lights

- ¾-inch (19-mm) screws

- circular saw

- precut mirror, 23×15 inches (58⅜×38 cm)

- mirror hangers, as needed

- hammer

- 1-inch (25-mm) finishing nails

- Phillips screwdriver

- light switch, box, and cover

- power point socket

Instructions

1. Unpack the RAST chest. Label the two side panels of the chest "G" and "N," and label two of the drawer fronts "L" and "M." Set aside for later.

2. Take the two sheets of plywood measuring 30 inches (76.5 cm) long and label them "A" and "B." These will form the new sides of the dressing table. If you require a taller table, adjust the height accordingly. Then, take the sheet measuring 3×⅝×11¾ inches (7.5×1.5×30 cm) and label it "F"; this will be a hairdryer holder. Measure the diameter of your hairdryer nozzle and drill a hole in "F" to fit. Mine was 2 inches in diameter.

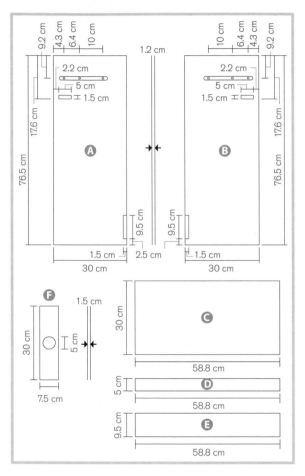

3. Take pieces "C," "D," and "E" from the RAST chest, unmodified. Screw "A" to "C" so they connect along the wide edge at a 90-degree angle, with "A" overlapping "C." In the same fashion, attach "B" to the other side of "C." "C" will act as the top of the table.

4. Using 1¼-inch (32-mm) screws, attach "E" vertically between "A" and "B," 1 inch from the

bottom of the table and flush against the back edges of "A" and "B." Next, attach "D" horizontally between panels "A" and "B," with "D," 7 inches below panel "C." Leave a margin of ¾ inch (2.2 cm) from the front edge of "A" and "B." Last, secure panel "F" to the side of panel "A" or "B," whichever is preferred. Align the ⅝-inch (1.5 cm) edge lengthwise against the panel, 7 inches from the top, and drill from behind "B" into "F" using 2-inch screws. Set aside.

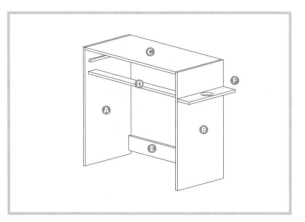

5. Get the front panel for the first drawer, which was not previously labeled. With a jigsaw, trim its width by 1 inch (2.5 cm) and then in the center of the panel, form a U-shaped drawer opening measuring 1¼×3½ inches (3×8.8 cm). Assemble the drawer according to IKEA® instructions. Set aside.

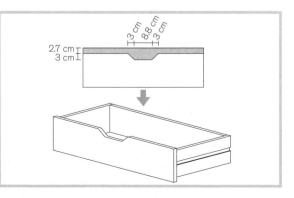

6. Locate the 2 pieces of plywood measuring 23×23⅛ inches (58.2×58.8 cm), which you should label "H" and "K," and the plywood sheet measuring 5¼×23 inches (13.3×58.2 cm), which you should label "J." On panel "H," use a hole saw to drill 4 2-inch (9-cm) diameter holes on each side, distanced 3½ inches from each other and 1 inch (2.5 cm) from the edges of "H." Then, wire the LED spotlights behind the panel.

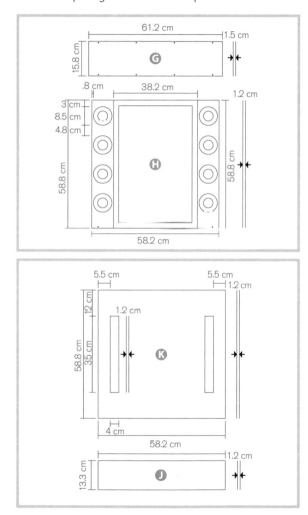

7. Attach the two boards measuring 1½×13¾ inches (4×35 cm) to "K" at about 2¼ inches from the sides and 4¾ inches (12 cm) from the top edge, using the short ¾-inch (19-mm) screws.

8. Using your circular saw, trim panel "G" to measure 6¼×24×⅝ inches (15.8×61.2×1.5 cm).

9. On the front of panel "H," install suitable hangers that you will later use to attach your mirror to "H." The mirror used for this project came with keyhole hangers on the left and right corners. We measured and marked the two spots for the screws and turned ¾-inch (19-mm) screws halfway into "H" for hanging the mirror. Once this is done, set your mirror aside. The diagram below shows how the mirrored box top comes together but do not assemble the mirrored box top at this stage. You will put it together in Step 13.

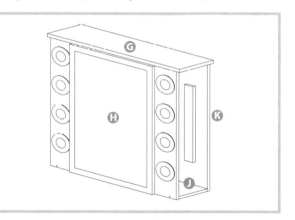

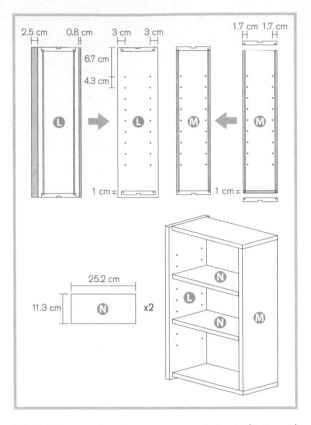

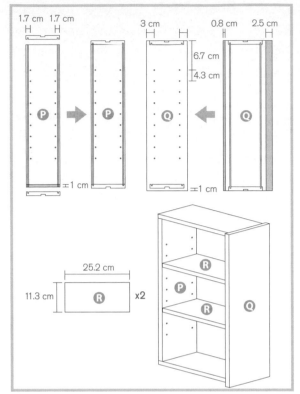

10. Using a circular saw, cut 1 inch (2.5 cm) from the top of panel "L" and shave ¼ inch off the bottom. Drill holes for dowels, leaving a margin of 1¼ inches (3 cm) on both sides, 2⅝ inches (6.7 cm) from the top and bottom, and 1¾ inches (4.3 cm) between dowel holes. Then, trim the short side of panel "M" to be ⅜ inch shorter so that the front panel of the drawer overhangs to cover the plywood base "J." On the bottom of panel "L," drill new pilot holes, 1/14 inch (2 mm) in diameter, ⅜ inch (1 cm) above the old ones, to insert the stem of IKEA®'s locking cam bolts. Trim the short edge of the provided drawer backing board by ¾ inch (1 cm). Assemble the drawer following assembly instructions.

11. Repeat Step 10 to make the right pullout drawer using panels "P" and "Q," but mirror the steps.

12. Using your circular saw, cut panel "N" into four pieces of the same size, each measuring 4⅜×10 inches (11.3×25.2 cm). Label two of these pieces "N" and two of these pieces "R." "N" will go inside pullout drawer "M," and "R" will fit inside pullout drawer "Q."

13. Butt the top edge of "H" against "G," forming a 90-degree joint. Use 1¼-inch (32-mm) screws to attach "G" to "H" at 4 points along "G," spacing about 7 inches between screws. "G" should overlap "H," but keep the edges flush. Then butt the long edge of "J" against "H" and attach similarly, with "H" overlapping "J," and drill from "H" into "J." Then lay the construction on a flat surface, with "H" facedown and "G" facing away from you.

14. Slot the 2 pullout drawers into the formed cavity, with pullout drawer "M" on the right side and pullout drawer "Q" on the left side. Cover the back of the opening with "K," with the drawer stoppers facing inside. Attach "K" to "G" at 4 points along the edge of "G," screwing into "K." At the bottom of "K," drill from "K" into "J" and attach with 1¼-inch (32-mm) screws.

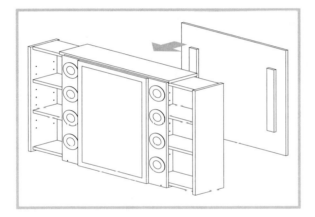

15. Align the mirrored box top on the tabletop "C," with the back and sides flush. Attach the mirrored box top to the table with screws, drilling upward from under the table. Then use a hole saw to make an opening through the tabletop "C" and base of the mirrored box top "J." Center this hole at about 11½ inches (29.2 cm) from the short

edge of "C." This is to allow the wires from the spotlights to escape the mirrored box top to the light switch plate on the side panel "B."

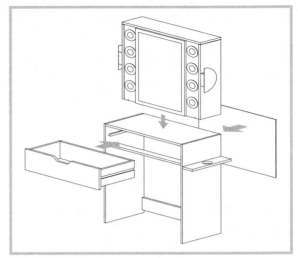

16. Get the backing board from the RAST chest and attach it to the back of the dressing table at the bottom, overlapping "C," "A," and "B." Use a hammer to fasten the board to the back with finishing nails.

17. Push in the plastic drawer runners that come with RAST and slot the drawer made in Step 5 into the predrilled holes on the sides of "A" and "B." You only need to install one pair of runners.

18. Fix the TOSTERUP handles onto the pullout drawers following assembly instructions.

19. Complete the wiring for the lights and power point for the hair dryer. Flip the switch, and let's dress up!

DOUBLE MURPHY BED

Bjørn Aksel Storaker

Oslo, Norway

Want a room for overnight guests but don't want to keep a dedicated guest room, especially when space is at a premium? Do what Bjørn did—he installed a Murphy bed in his home office for when the occasional out-of-towner drops by.

"We wanted a budget Murphy bed in a closet that does not take up too much space. There are many Murphy bed kits, but they are quite expensive, so we chose to go for a cheaper version. My version is slightly harder to pull up and down, but you can use it for training instead of weights," he says.

This hack is for a double bed and combines two PAX wardrobes, one that's 39³⁄₈ inches wide with two doors, and a second one that's 19⁵⁄₈ inches wide with one door. If you'd prefer a single bed, you can get away with using just one 39³⁄₈-inch wide PAX wardrobe frame.

IKEA® Home Furnishings

- 1 PAX wardrobe frame, 39³⁄₈-inch (100-cm) wide with two BALLSTAD doors
- 1 PAX wardrobe frame, 19⁵⁄₈-inch (50-cm) wide with one BALLSTAD door
- 2 LURÖY slatted bed bases

Materials

- handsaw
- fine sandpaper
- drill
- 1¼-inch (32-mm) zinc-plated screws
- stud sensor
- L-brackets
- 1 wooden beam, 3¼×1×53½ inches (8×2½×136 cm)
- tape measure
- double mattress
- two 2×4-inch (5×10¼-cm) pine boards, 51 inches (129½ cm) long
- two 2×4-inch (5×10¼-cm) pine boards, 83 inches (210¾ cm) long
- two 1½×2-inch (3¾×5-cm) pine boards, 78¾ inches (200 cm) long
- one 2×2-inch (5×5-cm) pine board, 78¾ inches (200 cm) long
- 2×4-inch (5×10¼-cm) pine boards, 57 inches (144¾ cm) long, as needed
- 4 door hinges, 4×4¼ inches (10×11 cm)
- 4 hinges for bed feet, 3×1¼ inches (7½×3½ cm)
- 2 magnets for bed feet
- two 4½-inch (114-mm) zinc-plated screws
- strap (optional)

Instructions

1. Construct the PAX frames according to assembly instructions. Once the wardrobes are completed, decide which sides of the wardrobes will attach to each other. On those two sides, use the handsaw to remove the inner walls, leaving the bottoms and tops of the frames intact. Use sandpaper to smooth the areas that have been cut.

2. Use one of the wall panels that was removed in Step 1 to attach the two frames to each other. Do this by placing the wall panel across the tops of the wardrobes, and every 11¾ inches, drill in the 1¼-inch zinc-plated screws.

3. The PAX wardrobe frames must be firmly secured to the wall using the materials included in the packaging to prevent the bed from crashing down unintentionally. Use a stud sensor to locate the studs behind the wall for the best possible grip. Then, use L-brackets to attach the 53½-inch beam to the top length of the wardrobe and to the wall as added support.

4. Next, work on the bed frame. Measure the width and length of the mattress with a tape measure to ensure that your pine boards are the right size for your frame; the double bed used for this project measured 51 inches wide and 78¾ inches long. Use the two 51-inch 2×4s for the top and bottom support beams, and the two 83-inch 2×4s for the left and right support beams; these will jut out an extra 2 inches on each side to form a butt joint. Secure the beams at the corners with screws.

5. To attach the LURÖY slatted bed bases, you will first have to secure support rails for the slats. First, make marks all along the inside of both side beams, 1 inch down from the top of the beams, and draw a line to connect these marks. Align the 78¾-inch 1½×2-inch boards with these lines, then use a drill to secure them with screws at 6-inch intervals. Then, mark the direct center on the inner edge of both the top and bottom beams, 1-inch down from the top of the beams. Align the 78¾-inch 2×2-inch board to these marks and secure with screws.

6. Use timber boards to level out the bottom of the wardrobe to give the bed enough room to open fully. This will also strengthen the base of the cabinet where most of the pressure will be concentrated. Stack two layers of 2×4s along the base of the wardrobe and screw them into the base. Make the second layer of 2×4s shallower than the first so that there is enough room between the base of the wardrobe and the doors. Also, be sure that when the bed frame is attached, it will be high enough for the bed feet to open fully and reach the ground.

7. Attach the bed to the 2×4s covering the base of the wardrobe frame using the 4-inch door hinges. Mount the hinges 9¾ inches in from the right and left walls of the wardrobe and 4 inches from the central door opening. Again, make sure the height of the base of the wardrobe frame is as

high as the bed feet and higher than the hinges for the wardrobe door.

8. With the bed frame open, place the LURÖY slatted base into the bed frame, resting it on the support rails. Secure the slats onto the bed frame with evenly spaced 1¼-inch zinc-plated wooden screws.

9. Place the bed feet at the end of the bed, on the corners farthest from the wardrobe. Attach the remaining hinges so one side connects to the bed frame and the other side connects to the bed feet. Add magnets on the side of the bed feet and on the bed frame, so when you pull up the bed, the feet will fold up.

10. Using the hardware that came with your PAX wardrobe, attach the doors to the wardrobe frame.

11. Attach the two 4½-inch screws to the top left and right sides of the bed, 7¾ inches from the top of the wardrobe frame, so that the bed will not fall out when in upright position. Drill holes for the screws so it is easy to remove them manually. You can also attach a strap under the bed to hold the linens in place when you move the bed up and into the closet.

12. When guests arrive, manually remove the long screws, and lower the bed carefully. The bed is a bit heavier than a regular Murphy bed kit, so it's best to get a partner to help you lower it or close it back up.

About the Contributor

As a true Scandinavian, both IKEA® and classic Scandinavian design are a part of Bjørn's DNA. Even though he's a big fan of classically designed pieces, he hacks because he can't find everything that he wants at retail stores. It's his way of getting "customized stuff that not everybody has." He lives in Oslo, Norway, in a townhouse with his wife and two sons. Having moved three times in five years, there's always something new to do. Catch his latest projects on his website, www.huskverna.com.

HEADBOARD STORAGE

Timothy and Mallory Barrett
California, United States

Timothy and Mallory Barrett live in a small but unique space overlooking the Pacific Ocean, so they try to max out the functionality of everything they own and use. They love their IKEA® BRIMNES bed frame and the storage space underneath, but with the bed set toward the window so they could take advantage of the ocean view, their heads were left in the middle of the room with no support. They needed a headboard, but the Barretts were not content with just any old headboard. They wanted something that would double as storage. It was a tall order, but this headboard hack lived up to it.

IKEA® Home Furnishings

- 2 sets TRONES 3-unit shoe storage bins
- BRIMNES queen-size bed frame with storage

Materials

- 5 natural 1×8-inch (2½×20¼ cm) hardwood boards, 72 inches (183 cm) long
- 6-inch (15¼-cm) circular saw
- 6 L-brackets, 1×1 inch (2½×2½ cm)
- hammer
- nails
- eight 1×6-inch (2½×15¼ cm) tongue-and-groove cedar fence boards, 72 inches (183 cm) long
- masking tape
- white paint
- paintbrush or foam paint roller
- drill
- 12 screws, 2 inches (51 mm) long
- 24 screws, 1 inch (25 mm) long
- 1 redwood 2×4-inch (5×10¼ cm) board, 9 inches (22¾ cm) long

Instructions

1. Stack the TRONES units, 3 wide and 2 high, to match the width of a fully assembled queen-size BRIMNES bed frame.

2. Use 4 pieces of 1×8-inch natural hardwood to frame the TRONES units on all sides. The top and bottom boards will overlap the side boards. For the top and bottom pieces, use the circular saw to cut the boards to measure 62½ inches. For the sides, cut the remaining 1×8-inch boards to measure 40½ inches. Nail all pieces together to form a rectangular box, screwing small L-brackets on the inside for ease of mind and extra stability. Note that this box should not perfectly frame the TRONES units; there should be room left over for the shelf you will create in Step 5.

3. Use the eight 1×6-inch tongue-and-groove cedar fence boards to give the bed-facing side of the TRONES frame some flare and warmth while adding a bit of structural support. Cut the boards to measure 60¾ inches so they fit flush within the newly formed frame. Nail the first board in place at the bottom of the frame, using two nails on each side of the headboard frame. Then, using the tongues and grooves as a guide, stack the next cedar board on top and nail it to the sides of the headboard. Continue this pattern all the way up.

4. Once the headboard is complete, tape off the cedar and paint the TRONES frame white to match the bed frame.

5. Drill pilot holes in the bed frame, and attach the headboard securely to the frame. For this project, it was secured in 12 locations: four rows of three 2-inch screws spaced evenly across the width of the headboard.

6. To create the additional open storage area above the TRONES units (which can become the perfect bookshelf for children's bedtime books), paint a 1×8-inch hardwood board to match the rest of the headboard and cut it to measure 60¾ inches, the same length as the cedar boards. You will use it as a small shelf. With the TRONES units in place, set the shelf board in place on top of the units and mark its location along the headboard. Remove the TRONES units, and then secure the shelf for a snug fit.

7. Stack the TRONES units in place to check the fit. The back of each unit has two slots for screw heads. With the TRONES units snug in place, take off the front of each unit, locate the holes, and drill in your 1-inch screws from the inside wall of the cedar boards.

8. The unit needs a vertical structural piece between the top frame and the small shelf. Cut a 2×4-inch piece of wood to measure roughly 9½ inches, squeeze it between the two hardwood boards, and nail it in from the top.

About the Contributors

Tim and Mallory love the tiny house lifestyle and thrive on natural design philosophies, often incorporating reused or salvaged materials into daily projects. The Barretts live in the Ocean Beach/Point Loma community of San Diego, California, over a two-car garage that looks down to the ocean. They have an outdoor "workshop" and a small yard packed tight with a hammock, vegetables, and native plants. Their space is home to Tim, Mallory, their daughter Florence James, and their dog Gulliver.

STRING-SIDED CABINET

Jules Yap and Martin Wong

Malaysia

The HEJNE has many predrilled holes. Many often complain the holes are an eyesore, but Jules and Martin thought, "What if we made use of these holes and created a hack around them?" From that thought, they gave birth to the string-sided cabinet. What they like best about this cabinet is the many, many ways you can tie it up. It's shoe lacing on steroids.

IKEA® Home Furnishings

- 4 HEJNE posts
- 4 HEJNE shelves, 30³/₈×18½ inches (77×47 cm)

Materials

- drill
- 6-mm drill bit
- measuring tape
- 180-grit sandpaper
- mallet
- jigsaw
- 1-inch (25-mm) nails
- hammer
- 300 feet (91 m) nylon string

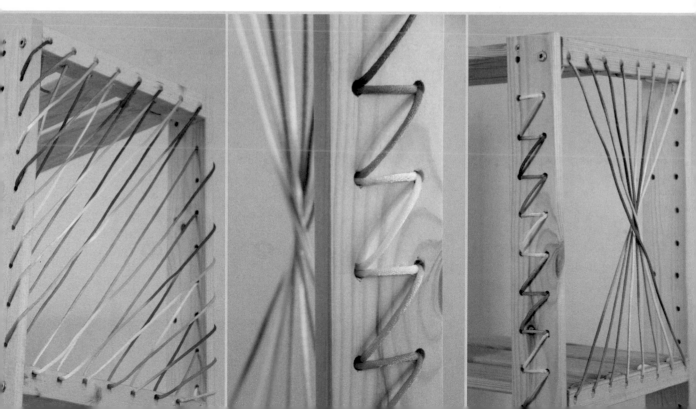

Instructions

1. You are in for a lot of drilling! On the 2 back posts, add 2 holes between each of the predrilled holes, leaving 1⅝ inches (4.2 cm) of space between each of the holes. You could add more, if desired.

2. On the 2 front posts, add 2 additional holes between predrilled holes but along the left and right edges (marked as "FL" and "FR" in the diagram) only. (See Fig. 1.)

3. For the top shelf "A," drill holes along the back. Leave 1⅝ inches (4.2 cm) between each hole and a gap of ½ inch to each edge. For the short sides, drill holes at a 45-degree angle, from the side to the bottom of shelf, leaving a distance of 1½ inches (3.8 cm) between each hole. (See Fig. 2.)

4. Repeat Step 3 for the bottom shelf "D," except for this shelf, drill at a 45-degree angle from the side to the top of the shelf. (See Fig. 3.)

5. Use sandpaper to smooth the holes. (See Fig. 4.)

6. The 2 middle shelves "B" and "C" need to be shortened so as not to obstruct the flow of the strings. The HEJNE shelf is made out of 5 horizontal boards held together by nails fastened on a side ledge. Hold the side ledge and, using a mallet, knock the horizontal boards from behind to loosen them from the nails. Repeat on the other end.

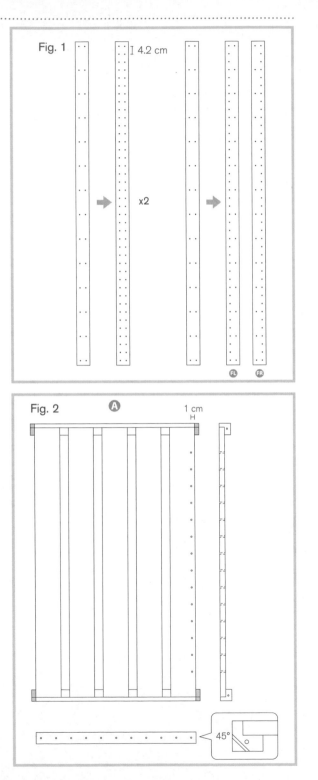

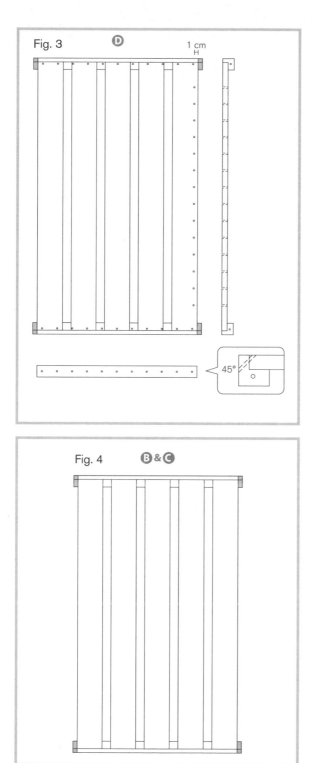

7. Using a jigsaw, shorten the 5 boards by 2½ inches (6.3 cm). Then, nail them back with a hammer onto the side ledge, spacing them out equally. (See Fig. 5.)

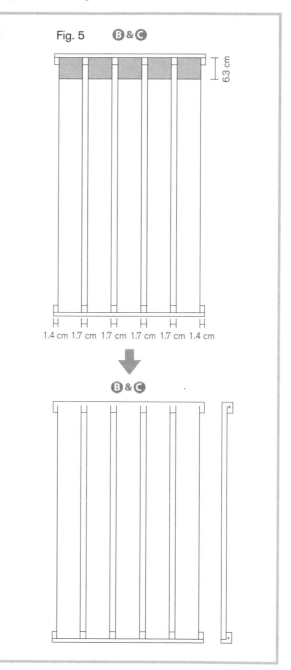

8. Construct the HEJNE rack according to assembly instructions, except for the 2 middle shelves, which should be bolted into the inner predrilled hole, rather than the outer hole. (See Fig. 6.)

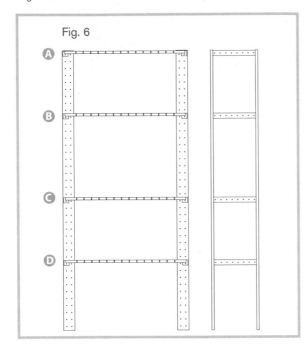

Fig. 6

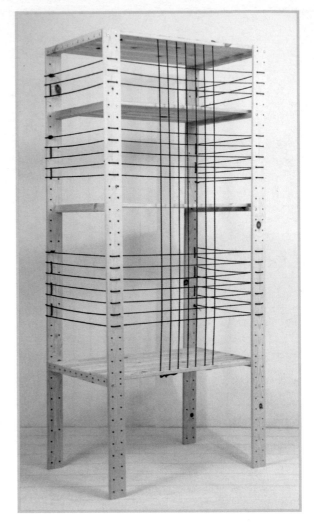

9. Loop your string through the eyelets. We used a multicolored fluorescent nylon string. You can create any pattern you like.

To make a smaller version:

10. You can also make a variation for the shallower HEJNE using the 30³/₈×11-inch (77×28 cm) shelves, letting you make shorter loops. To do this, repeat Steps 1 and 2 on the posts. Drill holes along the back of the top and third shelves, "A" and "C." For the sides, drill at a 45-degree angle, from the side to the bottom of shelf. (See Fig. 7.)

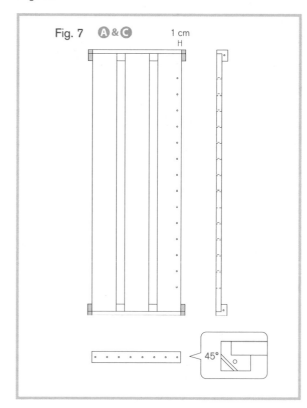

11. For the second and last shelves, "B" and "D," drill holes along the back at a 45-degree angle, from the side to the top of shelf. There is no shelf shortening required. (See Fig. 8.)

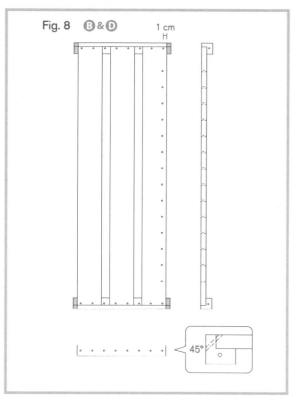

12. Assemble the HEJNE according to Fig. 6 on page 52.

13. Loop in the strings, and you're done!

MALM CHEST WITH PULLOUT LAPTOP TABLE

Otis Kotsanos

United Kingdom

Renting a beautiful attic conversion (complete with skylight and Juliette balcony) on a London Victorian house is as lovely as it sounds, but adding two wardrobes and two MALM chests left no room for a desk. Otis soon realized he really needed a space to work and write, and the final product had to be freestanding, yet safe and durable. At last, he came up with the winning idea of a pullout laptop table between the top two drawers of the MALM, which is at the perfect height for a desk. The TERJE folding chair and MALINDA cushion work great with this hack. They can be folded and stored under the bed when not in use.

IKEA® Home Furnishings

- MALM chest

- UTRUSTA kitchen cabinet shelf, 31½×14½ inches (80×37 cm)

Materials

- handsaw
- bottom-mount drawer slides for the pullout table, 17¾ inches (45 cm)
- ¾-inch (19-mm) screws

- tape measure
- screwdriver
- pencil
- handle (optional)

Instructions

1. Remove all drawers from the MALM chest.

2. Cut the brace between the top two drawers in half.

3. Looking from the inside, loosen the brace by turning the two connecting screws counterclockwise. Both sides of the top brace can now be pulled out.

4. You should be left with the metal and wood dowels, as shown below. Unscrew the metal bit but leave the wooden dowel in place.

5. Start by adding the left drawer slide. Rest it on top of the wooden dowel and position it as shown below so that the drawer slide is on the very edge of the MALM side panel.

6. Mark and add the first screw.

7. Mark and add the remaining screws to attach the slide to the inside of the unit, as shown below. They must be screwed in as tight as possible, as any protrusion can cause the drawer to get stuck. Remove the wooden dowel.

8. Repeat on the right hand side.

9. The UTRUSTA shelf is longer than the opening in the MALM frame and will need to be cut to fit. To get the right width, fit the inner drawer slides on to the UTRUSTA shelf and measure. For this project, the shelf was cut to $29^3/_8$ inches at a local hardware store. This may vary depending on type and size of chosen drawer slides.

10. Use the long wood screws included with the IKEA® packaging to secure the drawer slides to the shelf.

11. Slide the laptop table in place. You may add a handle if you wish, or leave it alone for a minimal look. Once the laptop table is in, replace the drawers. The top drawer goes in last.

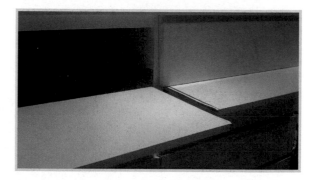

12. For safety, anchor the MALM units to the wall with the provided wall-mounting kits to prevent a tip over.

About the Contributor

Otis is an IT support administrator by day. He loves tweed, whiskey, photographs of red deer, and traveling to the Scottish Highlands. When not stuck in front of a computer, he can be found in the kitchen making really good sushi! He offers a big thanks to Frank "for driving me to every single IKEA® trip in the last two years."

BUILT-IN HOME OFFICE

Thomas and Katie Musser

California, United States

The Musser family is all about DIY on a budget. They make furniture to meet their needs while fitting the décor of the home.

"We have a room in our home we like to call the Cropice. It serves as craft room, playroom, and office. It was in desperate need of organization, specifically shelves. I really like the built-in look, but not the cost," says Katie. "I saw a pin on Pinterest that used the IKEA® BILLY bookshelves to create a built-in look by adding molding and framing. That gave us the idea to start with the IKEA® shelves, build them up, and add a desk in the middle."

IKEA® Home Furnishings

- 2 BILLY bookcases, 31½×11×79½ inches (80×28×202 cm)

Materials

- 4 plywood boards, 1×8 inches (2½×20¼ cm)
- drill
- countersink drill bit
- screws
- measuring tape
- circular saw
- one 8-foot (244-cm) sheet pine plywood, 48×¾ inches (122×1⅞ cm)

- one 8-foot (244-cm) sheet pine plywood, 24×¾ inches (61 ×1⅞ cm)
- paint
- paintbrush or foam paint roller
- plywood boards, 1×4 inches (2½×10 cm), as needed
- L-brackets
- strips of decorative molding, 1×2 inches (2½×5 cm) (optional)
- crown molding (optional)

Instructions

1. Assemble the BILLY bookcases according to IKEA® instructions. Place the bookcases flush against the left and right sides of the room, in the corners.

2. Trim two 1×8s to measure 32½ inches and two to measure 12 inches.

3. Using a countersink drill bit, attach the 32½-inch boards in front of each BILLY. The boards should be flush with the floor. On the left bookcase, the board should extend 1 inch to the right, while on the right bookcase, the board should extend 1 inch to the left.

4. Using a countersink drill bit and screws, attach the 12 inch boards on the side of the bookcases so that they are flush with the floor and with the overhanging edges of the 32½-inch boards.

5. To determine the correct measurements for the top portion of the frame, measure the height of the room, then subtract the height of the bookcases from the height of the room. This will be your top frame height. Next, use your circular saw to cut the pine plywood into two panels measuring 32½ inches × top frame height and two panels measuring 12 inches × top frame height, for a total of four panels. Add an extra 2 inches to the height of these panels so they overhang the bookcases.

6. Using a countersink drill bit and screws, attach the 32½-inch and 12-inch panels that were cut in Step 5 to the top of the BILLY bookcases so that they mirror the panels at the bottom.

7. Paint the bookcases and plywood in a matching shade.

8. Attach the bookcases to the wall using L-brackets.

9. To make the desk, cut the remaining pine plywood to fit the space between the bookcases. Fit 1×4s around the edges and top of the plywood to make a thicker desk. Paint to match.

10. Optionally, attach 1×2-inch strips of decorative molding to the sides of the BILLY bookcases for a luxurious built-in look, and attach crown molding to match the rest of the room. Paint to match.

About the Contributors

Thomas is really into woodworking, which has helped in IKEA® hacking. He belongs to a club called SoCal Woodshop, and the guys in the group help each other out with projects. Katie loves decorating and being creative. Usually she'll come up with the ideas and Thomas makes them happen (or tells her it's not going to work). With the little ones and only one of them working, they have to be creative and frugal in remodeling. IKEA® is always a great option for home improvements because it's so affordable.

The Mussers live in Los Angeles, California, with a one year old, Brendon, a four year old, Gracen, and a loveable yellow Labrador named Nilla Wafer.

BOOKSHELF SOFA TABLE

Jochem Cooiman

The Netherlands

Jochem and his family bought a large orange sofa. They decided that the best place for it was in the living room with its bright orange back showing. "We do love orange, a typically Dutch color, but not to this extent," says Jochem. "Besides the overly beaming color, our old BILLY bookshelves were standing too close to the new sofa. 'What if the smaller BILLY wasn't there? Could we actually drop it on its side?' we then asked ourselves." He got the idea that by adding wheels underneath the bookcase and placing a painted cover on top, they would end up with a stylish, one-of-a-kind sofa table and room divider.

IKEA® Home Furnishings

- BILLY bookcase, 15¾×11×78¾ inches (40×28×200 cm)

- BILLY extension, 13¾×11×15¾ inches (35×28×40 cm) (optional)

Materials

- wood glue or all-purpose glue
- screwdriver
- 2½-inch (64-mm) flathead screws
- 4 or 5 rotating wheels/casters
- 16 self-tapping screws, 1 inch (25 mm)
- MDF side panel, 11×1×79½ inches (28×2½×202 cm); 11×1×93 inches (28×2½×237 cm) if using extension
- 2 MDF side panels, 15×1¾×11 inches (40×2½×28 cm)
- 1-inch (25-mm) flathead screws
- sandpaper
- paint
- paintbrush and foam paint roller
- 1½-inch (38-mm) flathead screws

Instructions

1. Lay the bookcase on its side. Use the 2½-inch screws to secure the shelves to the BILLY by screwing through the side of the BILLY into the shelves.

2. Optionally, if you choose to use the extension, use all-purpose glue or wood glue to attach the extension to one of the short sides of the BILLY bookcase frame. Then, secure the extension by diagonally screwing four 2½-inch flathead screws into the extension from inside the BILLY, each approximately 1 inch from the edge.

3. Connect four casters to the side of the bookcase that you choose to use as the base, using the 16 self-tapping screws. Attach a fifth caster if you are using the BILLY extension.

4. Lay the long MDF panel on the floor and align the edges of the two shorter panels with those of the longer panel at 90-degree angles. Before gluing, check to make sure the panels will fit over the BILLY. Then connect the edges with wood glue.

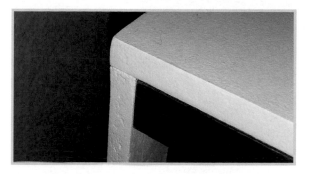

5. After the MDF panels have dried for an hour, sand the panels, particularly the joints between the long and shorter panels.

6. Paint the MDF in your desired color. Optionally, add a second or third layer of paint.

7. Place the painted MDF frame over the bookcase. Secure the panels to the bookcase by using all-purpose or wood glue and drilling in four 1-inch flathead screws from inside the bookcase.

8. Roll it to where you want it and voilà, you're done!

About the Contributor

Jochem lives just north of Rotterdam, The Netherlands, with his wife and two kids, in a terraced house. When he's not hacking, Jochem works for the municipality of Rotterdam as an advisor in innovation. His other interests include science fiction novels (particularly those by Asimov, Herbert, Heinlein, and Orwell). Asimov's way of envisioning the future, with new technology and new social and political orders, fascinates him. Creating an IKEA® hack is at least one small step that he can take in that direction.

EASY TV UNIT

Jules Yap and Martin Wong

Malaysia

The LACK side table was meant for bigger things. In this case, Jules and Martin made it work as a TV unit.

IKEA® Home Furnishings

- **2 LACK side tables**

Materials

- Phillips screwdriver
- penknife
- jigsaw
- pencil
- drill
- countersink drill bit
- ½-inch (13-mm) screws
- 3 pieces plywood, 54×¾×19½ inches (137×1¾×49½ cm)
- circular saw
- coarse- and fine-grit sandpaper
- primer
- paint (white)
- foam paint roller
- dry cloth
- 6 L-brackets, 1¼ inches (3 cm) (optional)

Instructions

1. Unpack the first LACK table and construct it according to assembly instructions. Each leg screws up to a point where you won't be able to turn it in any more. Note which legs screw into which corners. Then, unscrew the legs.

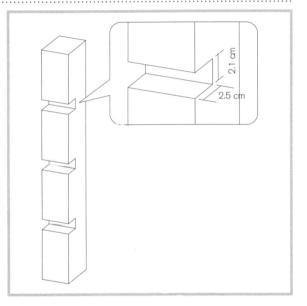

2. On the inside of each leg, you will need to make 3 dado cuts of approximately 1 inch (2.5 cm). This is where you will later slot in the plywood shelves. Measure 3⅛ inches (8 cm) from the top of the leg to find the top of the first dado, and mark 1 inch (2.5 cm) after that line for the width of the dado cut. Then measure 3⅛ inches (8 cm) from the bottom of the first dado to find the second dado, and again leave an inch of space to make the cut. Repeat once more to make the third dado marking. Make sure the cuts match on all legs.

3. Score the dado cut lines with a penknife to reduce the chances of the veneer tearing off. Use a jigsaw to make the dado cuts, cutting straight sides first and then diagonally trimming down the material until you have nice dados.

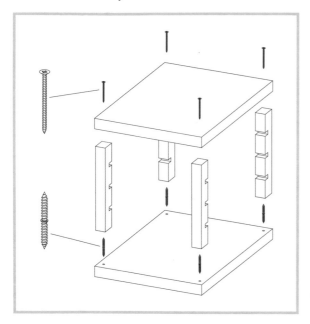

4. Once you've made all the dado cuts, turn your attention to the end of the leg without a predrilled hole. With a pencil, draw an X that touches all four corners of the end of the leg. Drill a pilot hole into the center of the X. Repeat on all 3 legs.

5. Screw the legs back into the tabletop, following your earlier note of where each leg should go.

6. Unpack the second LACK table. You'll be using the tabletop only. With the underside of the table facing upward, set the second tabletop on top of the first table's legs. Countersink ½-inch screws into the four corners of the second tabletop to attach it to the 4 legs, aligning your screws with

the holes you drilled in Step 4. Then, flip it over and set it aside.

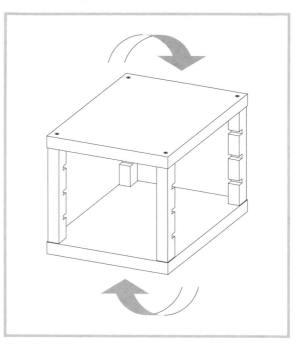

7. Measure the distance between two corresponding dado cuts and cut your plywood to fit. Ours was 19½ inches (49.7 cm). We used a circular saw to get a straight edge. If you don't have one, you can still use a jigsaw to cut the plywood.

8. Sand the plywood down, starting with the coarse-grit sandpaper and finishing with the finer grit for a smooth feel.

9. To paint, use a dry cloth to wipe off the sawdust. Then use a foam roller to apply the primer, following the grain of the plywood. Let it cure for 24 hours. Lightly sand the plywood again with the fine sandpaper, then wipe clean with dry rag. Finish with the paint of your choice, always painting in the direction of the grain. You may need to apply two coats. Allow the paint to dry thoroughly between coats.

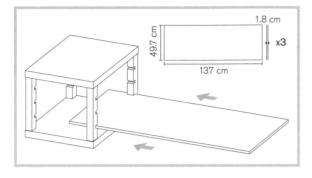

10. Slot the plywood shelves into the dado cuts. It should be a snug fit, but if you want additional security, screw in L-brackets with ½-inch screws to hold the shelves to the legs.

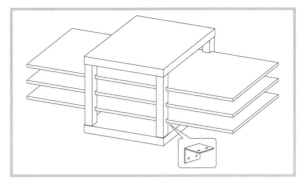

JUNIOR DOUBLE LOFT BEDS

Ana Romero

France

The transition from kindergarten to school for Ana's two daughters required some urgent adjustments to their tiny bedroom. The only solution was loft beds with study spaces underneath; however, the standard-sized beds could not fit into their bedroom, which was only 29½ square feet (9 square meters). Ana had to decide between calling in an expensive carpenter or hacking some IKEA® furniture. So, while her husband was abroad for a week and her three children were asleep, she went for it. The best part of the IKEA® hack was that she did not need to get rid of her children's old KRITTER beds; instead, she just up-cycled them.

IKEA® Home Furnishings

- 2 KRITTER beds
- 1 KALLAX shelving unit
- 2 MICKE desktops (optional)
- 2 SKÅLBERG/SPORREN chairs (optional)

Materials

- handsaw
- drill
- 68 screws
- four 1¾×2¼-inch (4³/₈×5¾-cm) planks, 62½ inches (159 cm) long
- four 1×2¼-inch (2½×5¾-cm) planks, 30½ inches (77½ cm) long
- four 1×2¼-inch (2½×5¾-cm) planks, 67 inches (170 cm) long
- four stainless steel angle brackets, 3½×2¾ inches (9×7 cm)
- 4 angle brackets, 2×2 inches (5×5 cm)
- paint
- paintbrush or foam paint roller
- prebuilt ladder, approximately 67×15¾ inches (170×40 cm)

Instructions

1. Saw the legs off on the foot side of both KRITTER beds, which is the side that will be resting on top of the KALLAX shelving unit. You do not need to remove guard rails from the KRITTER beds, if they are being used, but you can, if you'd like.

2. Next, cut out a 1×15½-inch-long notch from the tip of each of the four 62½-inch wooden planks. This is where you attach the KRITTER bed's head-side legs, as well as the upper joists. On the same side that the first notch was taken from, measure 29½ inches from the bottom and cut out a 1×2¼-inch piece of wood; this is where the lower joists will attach.

3. With the help of a friend, connect two of the long planks by screwing one of the 30½-inch-long wooden joists to the bottom of the notches cut into the tops of the 62½-inch planks.

4. For one of the beds, attach the KRITTER bed legs to the long planks by screwing them into the joist. Use 5 screws on each side.

5. In order to keep the long legs sturdy, screw a second 30½-inch horizontal joist into the lower notches of the long planks.

6. Repeat Steps 4 and 5 for the other bed frame.

7. Use 3½×2¾-inch steel brackets to attach the two KRITTER beds on top of the KALLAX shelf.

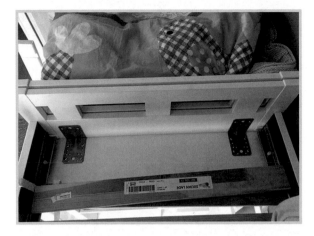

8. In order to make the construction more rigid, build a frame by connecting four 67-inch wooden joists between the wall-facing side of the KALLAX unit and the bed frames. The 67-inch joists should line up with 31½-inch joists that were used to connect the leg planks. Secure the frame with the four angle brackets in the corner of the horizontal joists. Repeat this process for the other bed.

9. Paint all the new parts white to match the KRITTER beds. Let dry.

10. If you'd like, trim the bottom edges of the ladder so it will lean on the floor at an angle. To make a hook for the ladder so that it could hang between the beds, bend a steel bracket, tape it up with white electrical tape, and attach it with two screws onto the ladder.

11. Optionally, add two MICKE desktops and SKÅLBERG/SPORREN chairs to complete the new bedroom set-up.

About the Contributor

As a Swede living abroad for eight years now, Ana enjoys hanging out in IKEA® from time to time just to get some Scandinavian air in her and be inspired by fun fabrics, bright and clean furniture, and practical solutions. She lives in Saint Cloud, a small community on the west of Paris with spectacular views of the Eiffel Tower, in a small apartment with her husband and three children.

CORNER BOOKCASE

Kevin Kovaleski

Arizona, United States

The corner of Kevin's front room was looking super sad and it stayed that way for five months, until his patience eventually ran out. Having just purchased a new house, he tried to find a bookshelf solution that softened the corner, but couldn't find a 90-degree bookshelf that didn't put a serious dent in his bank account. It was time for an IKEA® hack. The plan was to wrap two BESTÅ bookshelves with high-quality plywood to give them a custom look with a continuous top.

"I also love how the stain on the plywood perfectly matches my vintage pair of 1970s Dynaco speakers from Denmark," says Kevin.

IKEA® Home Furnishings

- **2 EKBACKEN countertops (optional)**
- **2 BESTÅ frames, 25¼×15¾×47¼ inches (64×40×120 cm)**

Materials

- 8-foot (244-cm) plywood board, 48×¾ inches (122×2 cm) (optional)
- measuring tape
- circular saw
- pre-stain
- stain
- satin polyurethane
- foam paint roller
- paintbrush
- wood glue
- 10 clamps
- drill
- countersink bit
- screws

Instructions

1. Construct two IKEA® BESTÅ bookshelf frames according to assembly instructions.

2. Get a piece of plywood from your local wood-workers' store, or two EKBACKEN countertops from IKEA®. Use the circular saw to cut the wood or countertops into two panels measuring 27¼×15½ inches and two panels measuring 53×15¾ inches.

3. On both of the 53-inch-long panels, measure 15¾ inches from one of the short edges and mark the point of measurement. Use a straightedge to draw a line from the mark to the opposite corner. Cut the panel at a 45-degree angle along the line. You should wind up with an edge measuring approximately 22¼ inches.

4. Do a dry fit to make sure that all your measurements are accurate before staining. The two long boards should fit on top of the BESTÅ frames with the angled edges resting snugly in the corner. If your wall is not a perfect 90-degree angle, you may need to trim the panels to fit. The sidepieces should overhang the bottom of the BESTÅ frames and top pieces.

5. Following the directions provided on the products you've chosen, cover the wood paneling with pre-stain, wood stain, and satin polyurethane using a foam roller and a paintbrush for the edges.

6. When the stain dries, secure the plywood pieces to the BESTÅ using wood glue.

7. Clamp the plywood pieces to the bookshelves and countersink screws from the inside of the bookshelf into the underside of the plywood. Space your screws evenly for a tight fit.

About the Contributor

Kevin and his wife live in a single-family home in Tempe, Arizona. They try to strike a balance between interior design that is true to the rustic, Southwest vibe while decorating with modern furnishings. Beyond this IKEA® hack, the Kovaleski home is almost entirely furnished with vintage, designer furniture that they've collected from treasure hunting on Craigslist. Beyond the occasional IKEA® purchase, they don't believe in buying new furniture. Kevin feels vintage furniture is made with better materials through smaller-scale manufacturing. So, even in how they source their furnishings, the hacking spirit is very much alive.

MID-CENTURY–STYLE MEDIA CABINET

Meera Pendred

United Kingdom

Meera needed a cabinet for DVD storage but struggled to find one that fit her narrow alcove. She knew the style she wanted. Her inspiration photos all had a similar theme: wooden doors, white outer frame, slim black handles, and mid-century-style splayed legs. So she started looking at IKEA® products for a cabinet that would come close to her requirements. The METOD kitchen wall unit was the perfect size and she loved the rough-sawn oak texture of the HYTTAN doors. In areas where METOD is unavailable, the SEKTION kitchen unit is a suitable replacement, though the cover panel and door dimensions may need to be adjusted to fit. "The unit is perfect for my style and storage requirements. Besides that, I love that my friends have commented (unprompted!) that it is a lovely cabinet," says Meera. "And they were always surprised when told that I made it from a kitchen cabinet!"

IKEA® Home Furnishings

- METOD wall unit, 31½×31½ inches (80×80 cm)
- HYTTAN doors

Materials

- tape measure
- 2 cover panels in gloss white, 15×¾×31½ inches (38×1¾×80 cm)
- 2 cover panels in gloss white, 15×¾×33 inches (38×1¾×83½ cm)
- drill
- 2-mm and 4-mm drill bits
- work bench
- pencil
- 1¼-inch (32-mm) wood screws
- Phillips screwdriver
- 2 slim black handles of choice
- splayed furniture legs of choice

Instructions

1. Assemble the METOD unit with HYTTAN doors according to assembly instructions. Do not add the shelves yet.

2. Remove the doors to make it easier to attach the cover panels to the unit. Use the longer panels for the top and bottom of the unit and the shorter panels for the sides. Measure the unit before attaching the panels, ensuring the edges of the doors will be boxed in within the frame.

3. Locate the predrilled holes on each side of the unit where the door hinges typically attach. There will be two rows of holes on the top and bottom of each side panel. You will use the second row of pilot holes to attach the cover panels. For each side of the unit, drill through these 4 holes to the other side using an electric drill with a 4-mm woodworking drill bit.

4. Rotate the unit so that one of the sides is facing up. Place one of the side cover panels on top of it, making sure the top, bottom, and back of the unit line up exactly with the panel. With a pencil, make marks on the cover panel to match the 4 holes that you drilled.

5. Remove the side cover panel from the unit and place it on a workbench. Using a 2-mm woodworking drill bit, drill pilot holes exactly in the center of the 4 markings.

6. Rotate the METOD unit so that the other side is facing up and repeat Steps 4 and 5 for the other side cover panel.

7. Set the unit upright again and make 4 markings on the top of the unit, 2 inches from the front and back and 2¾ inches from the sides. Drill through these marks using the 4-mm drill bit. These will be the points of attachment for the top panel.

8. Rotate the unit so that one of the sides is facing up again. Line up the corresponding side panel, carefully aligning the panel's pilot holes with the pilot holes drilled through the unit. Using 4 wood screws and the Phillips screwdriver, screw in the side panel firmly. Turn the unit to the other side and repeat for the other side panel.

9. Set the unit upright and line up the top panel with the top of the unit, ensuring that it aligns perfectly with the back of the unit and the side panels. With a pencil, make marks on the top

panel to match with the 4 holes you drilled in Step 7.

10. Remove the top panel from the unit and place it on a workbench. Using the 2-mm drill bit, drill short pilot holes exactly in the center of the 4 marks.

11. Place the panel on top of the unit, carefully aligning the new pilot holes to the predrilled holes on the unit. Using 4 wood screws and the Phillips screwdriver, screw in the top panel.

12. Place the bottom panel on a workbench. Measure and mark 4 holes on the bottom panel, 4¼ inches in from all the edges. Carefully drill through the bottom panel at these 4 points using the 4-mm drill bit.

13. Turn the unit upside down and place the bottom panel on the bottom side of the unit, aligning the bottom panel exactly with the back of the unit and the side panels. Mark through the 4 holes onto the bottom side of the unit.

14. Remove the bottom cover panel. Using the 2-mm drill bit, drill short pilot holes in the bottom of the unit, exactly in the center of the 4 marks.

15. Place the bottom panel back onto the unit and attach it to the unit using 4 wood screws.

16. With the unit still upside down, measure and mark where the 4 legs are to be fitted, making sure that the screws for the leg fittings are clear of the side of the unit. For this cabinet, the leg fittings were positioned 2¾ inches in from the front, back, and sides of the bottom panel.

17. Using the 2-mm drill bit, drill pilot holes where you marked, then screw in the legs with the screwdriver.

18. Turn the cabinet over, taking great care to lift it fully so that the weight of the cabinet does not bear down on the legs unevenly, as this could potentially damage the legs.

19. Secure the unit to the wall using fixings available for free from IKEA® to prevent any chance of the cabinet being pulled over.

20. Align the handles over the doors to get an idea of where to position them; this is a matter of personal preference. Measure where the fittings will be needed and mark these positions on the doors, then double-check that the markings will result in symmetrical handles on both doors.

21. Drill through the doors using an appropriate drill bit for the fittings provided with the handles, and screw them in.

22. Attach the doors to the cabinet according to IKEA® instructions provided with the doors.

23. Finally, insert the adjustable shelves at the desired positions according to IKEA® instructions provided with the unit.

About the Contributor

Buying a home ignited the creative spark in Meera. In a bid to create a beautiful and personal home on a budget, she found herself trying out things that she has never done before: sewing, crafting, giving old unloved furniture a new lease on life, and hacking store-bought items. The pursuit of creativity is now a way of life for her; that is, when she's not chasing her kids! Her style is still evolving and is inspired by her kids, nature, her roots in Kenya, and of course, the global creative community on the Internet. Meera lives in Nottingham, UK, with her husband and her two little boys. She shares her projects and inspirations over at instagram.com/artyhomestudio.

CABIN BED WITH HIDDEN DEN

Jane Taylor

England, United Kingdom

Jane's daughter was growing up and needed more space. But the room was relatively small, with a large low window making it tricky to put furniture in front of it. Jane liked the idea of raising the bed higher so she could have more drawers underneath it, instead of trying to fit even more furniture items into the small bedroom. She looked at scores of readymade cabin beds and mid sleepers, but none matched her needs. She found her solution by hacking the IKEA® NORDLI chests into a simple yet stylish cabin bed that would last her daughter for years. The best bit is that it offers a secret den behind the row of drawers. They were able to fit a camping mat, bedding and pillows, and a string of lights. Now, their daughter loves reading and sleeping in there instead of her bed! If NORDLI is not available at your local store in these sizes, you can mix and match between NORDLI and MALM options.

IKEA® Home Furnishings

- 2 **NORDLI** modular chests of drawers
- 1 **NORDLI** chest of 2 drawers
- **BEKVÄM** step stool

Materials

- tape measure
- pencil
- two $6^5/_8 \times 3/_4$-inch ($7/_8 \times 16^3/_4$ cm) wooden boards, $74^3/_4$ inches (190 cm) long
- one $6^5/_8 \times 3/_4$-inch ($7/_8 \times 16^3/_4$ cm) wooden board, $38^1/_4$ inches ($97^1/_8$ cm) long
- $3/_4$-inch (19-mm) flathead wood screws
- 12 L-brackets
- drill
- full bit set
- handsaw
- two 1×1-inch ($2^1/_2 \times 2^1/_2$-cm) boards, $74^3/_4$ inches (190 cm) long (optional)
- 35-inch (90-cm) wooden bed slats (optional)
- two $1^1/_2 \times 2^1/_2$-inch ($3^3/_4 \times 6^1/_4$-cm) wooden boards, 71 inches (180 cm) long
- four $1^1/_2 \times 2^1/_2$-inch ($3^3/_4 \times 6 \times 1/_4$-cm) wooden boards, $26^1/_4$ inches ($66^3/_4$ cm)
- one $3/_4 \times 2^3/_4$-inch (2×7-cm) wooden board, 71 (180 cm) inches long
- 3-inch (76-mm) flathead wood screws
- 1 plywood sheet, $45^1/_4 \times 3/_4 \times 78^3/_4$ inches (115×18×200 cm)
- MDF sheet measuring 48×$3/_4$×96 inches (122×18×244 cm)
- two $1^3/_4 \times 3^1/_8$-inch ($4^1/_2 \times 8$-cm) wooden boards, 59 inches (150 cm) long
- 8 wall anchor bolts
- all-surface quick-drying primer and undercoat
- quick-drying satinwood paint
- synthetic paintbrush, 2 inches (5 cm)
- mini gloss roller
- fine sandpaper

Instructions

1. Make a wooden frame for your single mattress. For the sides, use two $6^5/8 \times 3/4$-inch boards measuring 74¾ inches, and for the foot, use one board measuring 38¼ inches. This frame will suit a standard single bed measuring 74¾×35 inches. Attach the sides and end panel using ¾-inch screws and L-brackets. Leave the top end of the bed frame open, as this is where you will install the headboard.

2a. Optional step: If you wish to add a slatted base, screw 1×1-inch boards, 74¾ inches long, along both long sides of the wooden bed frame. These boards will support 35-inch wooden bed slats, which can be purchased from a retailer of choice.

2b. Position the three NORDLI chests (we chose a wide, narrow, wide configuration) in a row with the back edge of the drawers 28 inches from the wall. The drawer fronts should face into the room.

3. Build a ladder-style frame to act as a support for the bed frame, along with the NORDLI chests in front. Use the two 1½×2½-inch boards measuring 71 inches as the sides, and connect them by equally spacing the 26¼-inch-long boards between them. Screw the four boards in place with 3-inch flathead wood screws. Use L-brackets at each corner of the frame to give it extra strength. When completed, the frame will be the same height from the floor as the NORDLI drawers.

4. Use anchor bolts to secure the 71-inch-long board measuring ¾×2¾ inches to the wall, with its top edge at a height of 29½ inches from the floor. This support beam should match the depth of the baseboard, and will hold the ladder-frame ¾ inch away from the wall for an even fit.

5. Place the ladder-frame along the back wall, butting it up against the wall where the headboard will rest. Secure the frame along the back wall by screwing it into the baseboard and the support beam, using 8 cm flathead wood screws.

6. For the base of the bed frame, use a plywood sheet measuring 45¼×¾×78¾ inches. If needed, you can get the sheet precut or split into two sheets. Lay the plywood onto the drawers and butt it up against the back wall so that it fits flush with the front of the drawer units.

7. Use a screwdriver to secure the plywood by screwing it into the ladder-frame and the NORDLI drawers. On each side, use about 8 flathead wood screws, 4 to 6 inches apart.

8. For the headboard and side shelf, cut your MDF panel to the following specifications, or you can have it precut at the home improvement store.

For the headboard

- Front panel: 44½×¾×23¾ inches (113×1⁷/₈×60¼ cm)
- Top panel: 44½×¾×3¹/₈ inches (113×1⁷/₈×8 cm)
- Side panel: ¹/₈×¾×24½ inches (³/₈×1⁷/₈×62¼ cm)

For the shelf

- Top panel: 6³/₈×¾×74¾ inches (16¹/₈×³/₈×189⁷/₈ cm)
- Front panel: 11¾×¾×75½ inches (29⁷/₈×1⁷/₈×191¾ cm)
- End panel: 6³/₈×¾×11¾ inches (16¹/₈×³/₈×29⁷/₈ cm)

9. To construct the headboard, screw the top panel to the front panel, along the long side, at a right angle. Remember to countersink five or six holes before screwing the panels together. Attach the side panel where it aligns with the other two panels, also countersinking holes before attaching the panels. The side panel of the headboard will be flush with the fronts of the drawers.

10. Before constructing the shelf, screw the first 59-inch board flat down to the plywood base of the bed frame, making sure that the front edge of the board is 6³/₈ inches away from the back wall. Using anchor bolts, attach a second board flat against the back wall at a height of 11 inches above the plywood base of the bed frame. These boards will support the shelf.

11. Secure the top panel of the shelf to the wall support board and the side panel of the shelf against the base support board. Screw the two shelf panels together, making sure that the ends of the panels are flush against the headboard. Secure the shelf panels using L-brackets. Then, attach the end panel of the shelf where the side and front panels meet, making sure all the edges are flush. Be sure to countersink your screws.

12. Lift the bed frame into place and screw it to the headboard and plywood base. Make sure the frame is flush with the front of the NORDLI

drawer tops. Secure with additional L-brackets in the corners and flathead screws.

13. Fill and sand the countersunk screw holes. Then, use a 2-inch synthetic paintbrush and mini gloss roller to give the completed bed two coats of quick-drying primer/undercoat, followed by two coats of brilliant white quick-dry Satinwood. (I prefer this paint because it's solvent-free, non-yellowing, and the brushes can be cleaned using water.) Leave the recommended time intervals between additional coats of primer and paint.

14. Put the mattress in place, add an IKEA® BEKVÄM step stool, and you are finished!

About the Contributor

Jane's a creative soul who loves sewing, crafts, photography, writing, bargain hunting, and DIY. This is one of the reasons she left her job as a pharmacist in December 2015 after more than 20 years to pursue her love of writing and creativity. She lives in Nottingham, England, with her husband and two daughters. They have two guinea pigs and would love a dog, but so far have resisted the temptation to get one. All of her IKEA® hacks, home remodeling, and musings on life are featured on her blog, www.maflingo.com.

HANGING LAMP

Jules Yap and Martin Wong

Malaysia

The BUMERANG clothes hangers have pretty contours. It's a pity they are usually hidden behind all those clothes. This hack gives them the chance to step into the limelight.

IKEA® Home Furnishings

- 6 BUMERANG clothes hangers, without shoulder shapers

Materials

- pliers
- jigsaw
- ruler
- wood file
- 1 piece scrap wood, 4×⁵⁄₈×4 inches (10×1½×10 cm)
- compass
- protractor

- pencil
- drill
- 2-mm drill bit
- wood glue
- fourteen 1¼-inch (32-mm) screws
- electric cord
- socket
- bulb

Instructions

1. Using pliers, remove the hooks from the BUMERANG clothes hangers.

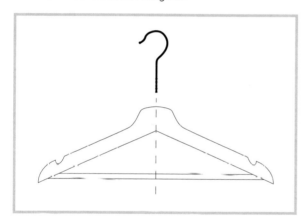

2. Cut the BUMERANG clothes hangers in half with a jigsaw. At the bottom of the neck of the clothes hangers, cut a 90 degree notch measuring ½×1½ inches (1.8×4 cm) so that it can rest on the circular lamp base you will create. Using the jigsaw, trim the bottom bar down by 1½ inches (4 cm).

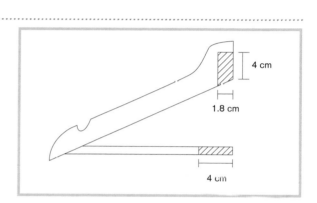

3. Check the cuts to make sure that they are square. If they aren't, file them down until they are 90 degrees.

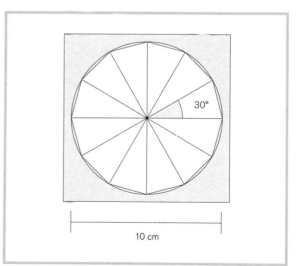

4. Get a scrap piece of wood and draw a circle with a compass, 4 inches (10 cm) in diameter. Draw a line down the middle of the circle and use a protractor to mark 30-degree sections on the circle. You should end up with 12 sections. Draw a line that connects the wide ends of the sections and cut the excess off (see shaded gray area in Fig. 3). You want a flat cross section for the BUMERANG clothes hangers to attach to. Cut this shape out with a jigsaw.

5. Drill a hole at the center of the circular base.

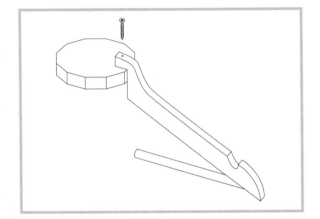

6. Drill holes at the top of the notched ends of the clothes hangers, ½ inch (1.8 cm) from the edge, for the screws to go through.

7. Drop a dollop of wood glue on the bottom of each notch before screwing the clothes hangers onto the circular base.

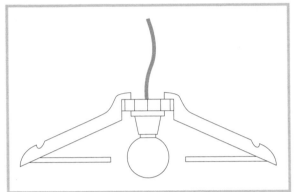

8. Thread the electric cord through the hole at the circular base and wire it to the bulb socket. Attach the socket to the base with screws.

9. Screw in your bulb, and shine on!

WORKING TOGETHER
DUAL WORKSTATION

Ritch Holben and Ken de Loreto

Miami, Florida, United States

Ritch and Ken wanted to create a 12-foot-long workstation for two that met their aesthetic requirements, given that it would be in their main living space. They also needed concealed storage. What they ended up with was a high-gloss, chrome beauty.

"The BESTÅ cabinets, with their glossy white finish, played off of the raw look of the bubinga wood top. Doubling the base with two sets of chromed legs raised the workstation to the right height and provided more airiness and storage," explains Ritch. "The top was custom-milled in the Berkshires with a raw edge left over for both look and ergonomics We chose the wood top to bring a piece of our Northern home into our new world of Miami. It ended up being a lot of look for a small price tag."

"It looked like a million bucks," Ken adds, "And when we sold the condo, the new owner bought it for more than we paid to create it. That's a clear sign of a great hack."

Unfortunately, IKEA® has discontinued the BESTÂ underframes, but you may be able to re-create a similar style with CAPITA legs or other legs in the BESTÅ range.

IKEA® Home Furnishings

- 3 BESTÅ base cabinets and doors
- 6 BESTÅ chrome underframes

Materials

- 24 L-brackets, 1 inch (2½ cm)
- screwdriver
- drill
- 1½-inch (38-mm) screws
- ¾-inch (19-mm) screws

- 2×12-foot ($^5/_8$×$3^5/_8$-meter) custom-milled wood slab top
- tung oil
- 12 self-adhesive non-slip pads, 4 per cabinet (optional)

Instructions

1. Construct each IKEA® BESTÅ cabinet according to assembly instructions. Leave off the back panels to allow for ventilation and cord management. To make up for the stability of the missing back panel, screw in L-brackets on the inside corners. The end cabinets would serve as individual storage, with the center cabinet being used for shared items such as a printer, computer router, and supplies.

2. Two sets of the BESTÅ underframes are required for each cabinet (one as the base and one on top) to raise the work surface to desk height. Rest the underframes directly on top of the BESTÅ cabinets, making sure they are perfectly aligned, and drill through from inside the cabinets to secure the underframes with the 1½-inch screws.

3. For the underframes below the cabinets, install per instructions from IKEA®.

4. For your countertop, place the 12 foot slab of wood or IKEA® countertop directly on top of the upper frames. No tools or mounting are required. If desired, use self-adhesive, non-slip pads to prevent the wood from slipping. Polish the countertop with tung oil.

About the Contributors

Ritch and Ken have been together for 18 years and married for 6. They split their time between two contrasting places called home: a 100-year-old farmhouse in the Berkshires, and a high-rise, modern condo in Miami Beach. In addition to keeping them out of the snow, their migratory lifestyle strikes a chord with their desire to balance rustic and modern. They share their lives with their two dogs Lucy and Oliver who, like them, are off-leash in the Berkshires and on-leash in Miami. Ritch's works can be viewed at www.RhDesign.me.

SUSPENDED SHELVING

David Meyer

Germany

David started his search for a new bookshelf, with this first choice being the BESTÅ system. But after some weeks of planning and searching the net, he came across the iconic George Nelson Wall-Unit and fell in love. Then he came to the conclusion that there was no affordable way to get one of those wall units in Germany. The only way to get something similar was to build his own.

If the STOLMEN posts are not available in your area, you can use the ELVARLI posts and brackets.

IKEA® Home Furnishings

- 5 STOLMEN posts
- 21 STOLMEN suspension fittings with 2 holders
- 14 STOLMEN end fittings
- 4 FYNDIG kitchen wall cabinets

Materials

- black spray paint
- measuring tape
- drill (optional)
- 6-mm drill bit for metal (optional)
- 40 aluminum L-brackets, 10×¾×2½ inches (25×2×6 cm)
- screwdriver
- ¼-inch (6.4-mm) screws
- level ruler
- 20 European spruce planks or similar materials, 31½×10 inches (80×25 cm)

Instructions

1. Spray paint the STOLMEN posts, fittings, and L-brackets black.

2. Mark an X on the floor where the first STOLMEN post should go. Then, use a tape measure to mark out a distance of 34¼ inches for the next post. This space is to fit the shelves and STOLMEN fittings. Repeat for all 5 posts. Install the posts according to assembly instructions.

3. The STOLMEN system relies on the fittings to join the components together. For this hack, the shelf rests on the fittings, butted by L-brackets to provide strength and stability to the shelf. Try to get brackets holes in the center. If these are not available, use a 6-mm drill bit for metal to drill holes to match the STOLMEN fittings.

4. Install the STOLMEN fittings to the posts at the desired shelf height using the included Allen wrench. For the first and last posts of your configuration, remember to use the STOLMEN end fittings, which each have only one holder. For the three posts in the middle, use the STOLMEN suspension fittings with two holders so you can secure both shelves and cabinets to the left and right sides of the post. See Step 7 for adjusting the STOLMEN fittings for cabinets.

5. For the shelves, screw a bracket to each short end of the shelf and place on top of the STOLMEN fitting. Use a level ruler to make sure that the shelves are flat and bolt them from below, from the fitting upward to the shelf. Repeat for the remaining shelves.

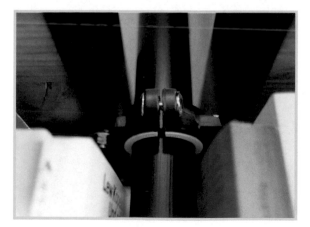

6. For the cabinets, first assemble according to assembly instructions. Then, use a screwdriver to secure an L-bracket to the cabinet, centering the bracket on the top of the short end of the cabinet. Repeat on the other side, and then on both bottom short ends.

7. To secure the cabinets to the posts, install the STOLMEN fittings on the posts to the left and right of the cabinet. Install them about 6 inches off the ground. Place the cabinet on top of these fittings, aligning the L-brackets to the fittings, and secure from below, like in Step 5. You may need someone to hold the cabinets in place as you bolt them in. Then, install the STOLMEN fittings on the left and right posts, aligning the fittings to the brackets on top of the cabinet. Bolt the fittings from the top down into the cabinet. Repeat until all 4 cabinets are up on the posts.

About the Contributor

It took David nearly four weeks to build his STOLMEN bookcase, but he loves the result. His advice to newbies would be to keep calm, be patient, and take enough time to plan. David lives with his family in Westphalia, Germany.

HEADBOARD AND PICTURE TREE

Jules Yap and Martin Wong

Malaysia

Their bed was without a headboard for years. At first, the plan was to use vinyl stickers with tree designs. Later, they thought they could easily make a tree-shaped headboard out of the HEJNE posts and shelves.

IKEA® Home Furnishings

- 6 HEJNE posts
- FISKBO photo frames in desired sizes

Materials

- measuring tape
- compass
- pencil
- jigsaw
- drill
- thirty ¾-inch (19-mm) screws
- wall plugs (optional)
- artwork and photos

Instructions

1. You will be using two of the posts to form the tree trunk (see Fig. 1). Measure 3 inches from one of the ends of the HEJNE post and mark it. Place the tip of your compass on this point and draw a curved line from the top of the HEJNE post toward the side. Cut off the edge with a jigsaw. Repeat for the second post.

2. Measure and divide the remaining four posts into 4 sections each, which would give you 16 sections of about 16½ inches (42 cm) each (see Fig. 2). Round the edges of each section so that they appear more branch-like, using the compass method described in Step 1. You could vary the length of the branches, if you want. Use a jigsaw to cut along the curved line.

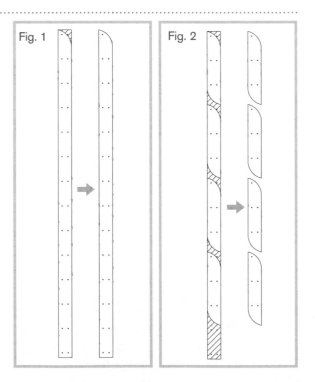

3. On the floor, lay out the trunk and the branches in a configuration that you like. Attach the branches to each other with screws. Do not attach anything to the trunk yet, and do not fasten the two pieces of the trunk to each other.

4. Using a drill, fasten each piece of the trunk to your wall using suitable screws and wall plugs, if necessary.

5. Transfer the branches from your layout to the wall, joining the branches to the trunk with screws. If your layout has wide spreading branches or your photo frames are heavy, it would be best to secure the branches to the wall as well.

6. Place photos and artwork in the FISKBO frames. Determine where you want to hang your photo frames. Drill in a screw at those spots and hang up the frames.

MUDROOM BENCH

Amy Taylor
Colorado, United States

When Amy went house hunting, she was sold on one when she saw an entire blank wall as she entered the house. The wheels immediately began to turn and she knew it was the perfect spot for a mudroom setup, where her family could stow away all their stuff in a decent-looking manner.

"Our previous home had a tiny entryway, with no place to put our things, and it drove me nuts. I like organization and the ability to hide clutter. I came across other IKEA® hackers who created a similar set up with TV benches, and I began looking for the right items from IKEA® that would accommodate our needs while remaining affordable. We ended up creating something awesome for less than $300."

Amy's DIY mudroom uses IKFA® STUVA storage benches for storing shoes, while also creating a handy place to sit. A DIY board and batten wall behind it forms a coat rack.

IKEA® Home Furnishings

- 2 STUVA storage benches
- 5 SVARTSJÖN hooks

Materials

- stud finder
- primer
- paint
- foam paint roller made for cabinetry
- drill
- screws in various sizes
- four 1×6-inch (2½×15¼-cm) tongue-and-groove pine boards, 72 inches (183 cm) long
- wood finish
- cloth
- polyurethane
- circular saw

- fine sandpaper
- one 1×4-inch (2½×10-cm) board, 72 inches (183 cm) long
- three 1×3-inch (2½×7¾-cm) boards, 96 inches (243 cm) long
- one 1×6 -inch (2½×15¼-cm) board, 72 inches (183 cm) long
- Kreg Jig
- 3 corbels, 4×5 inches (10×12¾ cm)
- nails and nail gun
- paintable caulk and caulking gun

Instructions

1. Put together the STUVA benches according to assembly instructions.

2. If needed, paint the benches to match the trim of your house. The best way to paint it is to spray it with primer first; one can will cover both benches. Then, paint it using a quart of your favorite paint and a foam roller made for cabinetry.

3. If you have baseboards where you want to place the benches, cut the boards away using a handsaw so that the benches fit snugly against the wall.

4. Screw benches into the wall studs. It helps to have a stud finder to find your studs, and screws at least 2 inches long for a secure attachment. Drill the screws through the back of each bench into the studs.

5. Stain the 1×6-inch tongue-and-groove boards in the wood finish of your choice. We used Minwax Honey 272 and applied it with an old rag. Once dry, apply two coats of polyurethane.

6. Using a circular saw, trim 1 inch from the width of one the tongue-and-groove boards to ensure all four boards fit the STUVA benches, as well as to get rid of the protruding groove. Sand the edge smooth.

7. Lay the tongue-and-groove pine boards on top of the benches and screw into the benches from underneath, using 1½-inch screws in about three places along the length of each board.

8. Cut the 1×4 to 71 inches. Cut the 1×3s into 12 pieces, six measuring 7 inches in length, and six measuring 34 inches in length.

9. Start by screwing in the 34-inch 1×3s vertically, directly above the bench. Space them 11 inches apart, with the first and last 1×3s flush with the edges of the bench. Secure the boards using a nail gun. Next, attach the 71-inch 1×4 on top of the 1×3s. Last, attach the 7-inch 1×3s vertically, directly above the 34-inch 1×3s.

10. Create a shelf by cutting a 1×6 board to 71 inches and attach to wall using a Kreg Jig and 2-inch screws screwed directly into the studs. The shelf should be flush with the 7-inch 1×3s at a 90-degree angle.

11. Hang corbels using the nail gun. Nail directly into the wall from above through the shelf. You may need to trim the corbels so they fit flush with the 1×3s and 1×6 used for the battens and shelf.

12. Caulk everything.

13. Paint board, battens, and shelf in desired paint color.

14. Hang SVARTSJÖN hooks using a drill and ½-inch screws on the horizontal 1×4.

About the Contributor

Amy now lives in Colorado, but originally hails from Michigan. She's a farm girl at heart, which is why she is drawn to the modern farmhouse style. She sells memory books and stationery for her line, Nuts & Bolts Paper Co. (nutsboltspaper.etsy.com) and blogs when she gets the chance. She works from home—in five-minute increments—due to the presence of her three little ones. After the purchase of their first house in April 2015, Amy's been working toward making it her dream home. Most weekends, she can be found working on a new project. Catch her latest projects on themombot.com.

BRICK COTTAGE DOLLHOUSE

Tamara Berg
California, United States

The BILLY bookcase is pretty ubiquitous, and Tamara has three of them in varying sizes in her home. "It practically cried out for personalization," she says. "I love the versatility and opportunity for individualization. Besides the brick cottage, I also made a cute little beach house with the BILLY bookcase. My next version will be a series of row houses. Imagine a little wrought-iron work...a front stoop...maybe lighting..."

IKEA® Home Furnishings

- BILLY bookcase in white, 41¾×11×31½ inches (106×28×80 cm)

Materials

- spray can of gray primer
- cellulose sponge
- serrated knife
- acrylic or water-based interior paint
- ceramic or plastic plate
- measuring tape
- pencil
- 1×12-inch (2½×30½-cm) pine board, 48 inches (122 cm) long
- MDF, 24×⅛×24 inches (61×³/₈×61 cm)
- circular saw
- drill
- 3-mm drill bit
- coarse-thread wood screws
- wood glue
- putty (optional)

- paintbrush or foam paint roller
- wide decorative trim molding, 48×¾ inches (122×2 cm)
- hot glue gun and glue
- picture frames for windows, 3×4 inches (7¾×10 cm)
- roll roofing material, 48×12 inches (122×30½ cm)
- 2×2-inch (5×5-cm) board, 8 inches (20 cm) long, cut at a 45-degree angle
- trellis fence, DIY or from craft store
- faux ivy, to fit
- ¼-inch (6-mm) thick foam core (optional)
- scrapbooking paper (optional)
- white glue or spray glue (optional)
- vinyl flooring (optional)

To make the brick walls

1. Apply gray primer to exterior sides of bookcase. Let dry.

2. To make brick detail, form a stamp by cutting cellulose sponge with a serrated knife to 4¼×1½ inches. Spread brick-colored acrylic paint spread out on plastic or ceramic plate. Add a few drops of chocolate brown to add dimension and variation in brick color. Dip sponge into paint to cover the stampface.

paint. Repeat until first row is complete. Re-apply paint as needed to fill any gaps or blank spots. To make next row, place sponge ¼ to ³⁄₈ inch above the top of the first brick line, and center the sponge above the "grout line" of one of the bricks from the first row. This will give your wall a staggered brick look. Continue with the rest of the row. Repeat until the bottom half of the house is covered in bricks. Let dry.

3. Beginning at the bottom of side of the bookcase, stamp the sponge to create first brick. About ¼ to ³⁄₈ inch away, apply another sponge stamp of

To make the roof

4. Cut the 1×12-inch board in two pieces, one at 24 inches long, and one at 23¼ inches long.

5. Drill one hole ⅜ inch from the edge of the 12-inch side of the 24-inch board, directly in the center. Drill two more holes, each 5 inches away on either side of this center hole.

6. Butt the shorter board up against the longer one at a perpendicular angle. Where the two boards meet, drill pilot holes through the existing holes into the end grain of shorter board.

7. Glue the two boards together, then secure with screws. Putty the holes if desired.

8. Prime and paint the roof panels with spray, roller, or brush.

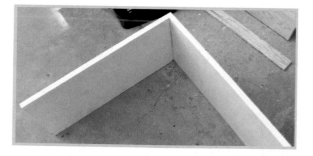

9. To create a fascia board, cut decorative trim molding and attach it to the front of the roof edge using hot glue.

10. Screw down through the roof into the bookcase where the roof meets the top corners of the bookcase. Use two screws per side.

11. To make back wall of attic area, take the 2×2-foot piece of ⅛-inch-thick MDF, draw a line connecting the corners diagonally opposite each other. Cut the MDF along that line, thereby bisecting the MDF diagonally and creating a triangle wall.

12. Attach to back of roof edge/attic, following the roof line, with glue or screws. If using screws, use 3 to 4 screws on each side, and drill pilot holes in the MDF and roof before securing.

13. Cut the roofing material to size, then adhere with hot glue.

14. To make the chimney, paint the 8-inch wooden 2×2 using the brick pattern. Attach to roof with screws.

Decorate the house

15. For windows, adhere picture frames using hot glue or screws, depending on the requirements of the frames.

16. Make your own trellis fence, or find one at a craft or hobby store. Secure to the house with glue and weave in faux ivy.

17. If creating interior walls, cut foam core to fit. If you cut the walls to be the same size as room ceiling height, you can simply push them into place and they will pressure-fit.

18. Optionally, use scrapbooking paper as wallpaper and floors. If available, use vinyl flooring scraps for floor. Attach with white glue or spray glue.

About the Contributor

Tamara lives in sunny Southern California in a condo with her handy husband. She also loves to hack food, fashion...pretty much anything she can get her hands on. Her favorite thing in the world is showing people how to make cool stuff and having them laugh while they learn. Some of her favorites can be seen on her show *The Tamara Twist* at www.youtube .com/user/TamaraCentral.

DISGUISED LAUNDRY BASKET

Marc Derveaux

Belgium

Sometimes, hacking happens when a lightbulb goes off in your head. That's what happened with Marc. "We wanted a clean bedroom and were struggling to find a place for our laundry basket. Having no space in our bathroom, we wanted to disguise it in our furniture," says Marc. "When we were at IKEA® looking for new drawers, I saw one that opened with hinges from the top. I saw an opportunity for converting it into my laundry basket." The best thing is, the basket is completely hidden. No one can tell that it holds dirty laundry. Here's how Marc did it.

IKEA® Home Furnishings

- **MALM 6-drawer chest with mirror**

Materials

- **electric saw**
- **wood panel, 23½×⅛×63 inches (65×¼×160 cm)**
- **screwdriver**
- **½-inch (13-mm) screws**
- **screwcovers**

Instructions

1. Assemble the MALM chest frame following assembly instructions. Do not add the top four drawers.

2. Assemble the top four drawers following assembly instructions. Do not include the bottom panels of the drawers or the planks that should be placed between the four drawers; these will be used later.

3. Using your electric saw, cut the large wood panel into four separate panels. You should wind up with one measuring 24½×12½ inches, two measuring 24½×16¼ inches, and one measuring 17×12½ inches. These will become the front panel, side panels, and back panel of the laundry basket.

4. On the two side panels, measure 6¾ inches from the bottom and make an incision ¾ inch high and 1½ inches deep so the laundry basket closes completely.

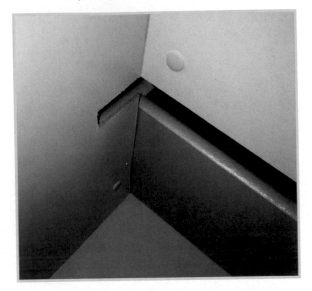

5. To make the laundry basket easier to open, reduce the length of the planks that come with the MALM unit by ¾ inch each. Attach the planks to the front panel at heights corresponding to the gaps between the four top drawers, using 3 screws for each plank. The planks should lay flat against the panel.

6. Insert the 4 joined drawers into their runners, as explained in the MALM assembly instructions.

7. Place the panel with the attached planks inside the drawers. The smooth side of the panel should be facing the back of the MALM unit. This makes it possible to open the four drawers at the same time, while keeping the front looking the same as the other MALM chests.

8. Use screws to attach the remaining 3 panels to the MALM unit to create a unified space. The two panels with incisions should be attached as side panels, with the incision at the bottom to allow for the brace of the MALM frame to slide in.

9. Attach the screw covers to prevent damage to clothing. This makes a clean laundry basket inside the MALM drawer.

10. Last, secure the chest to the wall with the provided restraints to prevent any tip-over accidents. Now, you just have to lift the top to dump in your dirty laundry. Pull out the joined drawers to empty the basket. Close it, and no one knows any better. Use the last two bottom drawers for additional storage.

About the Contributor

Marc and his wife, Noémi, don't shy away from rolling up their sleeves and getting their hands dirty—they've restored their home and made furniture for their growing family. They love to try new hacks, because, "What's the worst thing that can happen? Just buy a new IKEA® item if the project fails." Their can-do spirit has resulted in many easy, cheap DIY solutions. "It's part of how we are, and how we think." To get inspiration, Marc just walks around in IKEA®. If he can't find what he wants in the store, he'll make it. Marc, a nurse manager, lives in a little town in Belgium in a house with his wife and three children. Sharing their residence are a cat and three chickens.

ACKNOWLEDGMENTS

For a long time, I thought this book would be impossible. Now, at the tail end of writing, I look back, and I'm full of mixed emotions: thankful, excited, nervous, stressed, and relieved that I can soon get back to some semblance of life before the book. But one thing is certain: I'm glad we did this. And we did this together.

First of all, I want to thank the contributors to this book: Amy Taylor, Ana Romero, Antonio Tapia and Scott Vedder, Bjørn Aksel Storaker, Danielle Connelly, David Meyer, Gretchen Howard, Jane Taylor, Jochem Cooiman, Thomas and Katie Musser, Ken de Loreto and Ritch Holben, Kevin Kovaleski, Marc Derveaux, Meera Pendred, Otis Kotsanos, Sofia Clara, Tamara Berg, and Timothy and Mallory Barrett. You guys are awesome. Thank you for the patience with the edits and the endless back and forth, just to make sure that the end product would be good. I hope I did your projects justice. Without your contributions, this book would not be seeing the light of day. Thank you. (For more information on the contributors for this book, please visit www.ikeahackers.net/book-contributors.)

Next up, my partner-in-hacking, Martin Wong, who almost single-handedly conceived, hacked, photographed, and illustrated our seven hacks. You amaze me, again and again. You made our hacking days fun and fruitful. Also deserving special mention is our friend, Chan Ying, who generously lent us tools, equipment, space, and his truck to haul the goodies, and for turning up with packets of iced coffee when we needed it most.

The team at Ulysses Press, you rock. If you had not first reached out to me about this book, I would not have committed to it. Special thanks to Casie, who made everything go smoother, as well as Claire and Shayna, for their super editing skills and sharp eyes. The book is so much better because of you.

My assistant, Sharon Lim, who kept track of everything, almost right up to the delivery room: I couldn't have done this without you.

And I can't forget to thank my mom and sisters, who are my biggest fans and love me no matter what; my dad, though he's no longer here with us, who gave me the love for making things; and my crazy MAD Ladies and friends at Every Nation Church Damansara, who cheered me on when I was super-stressed and reminded me that I was still sane, compared to you guys.

To the contributors to IkeaHackers.net: Thank you for sharing your amazing hacks with me over the last 10 years. You didn't have to, but I'm so glad you did. Thank you for opening up your homes and workshops to the IH community.

Thanks to IKEA®, of course, for making furniture that we love to tear apart and rebuild. Keep doing what you're doing, and we'll keep hacking.

And most of all, to my Father God and Lord Jesus Christ, who sparked the lightbulb in me 10 years ago to start IkeaHackers. Thanks to Him, I get to be on this grand adventure. I look forward to the next with You.

ABOUT THE AUTHOR

Jules Yap is a creative soul at heart. As far back as she can remember, she has always been crafting, writing, and making things from whatever she could lay her hands on. Her creativity led her toward the advertising industry, where she clocked in as a copywriter and out as creative director, 15 years later. She founded IKEAhackers.net in 2006, which spurred the IKEA hacking movement and turned hacking into a home decorating staple. To date, her site houses more than 6,000 IKEA hacks, the largest collection of IKEA® hacks anywhere on the Internet. Her blog has been featured in leading home decorating websites, books, and magazines. She lives in Selangor, Malaysia, in a two-room apartment filled with IKEA® hacks. "My home is full of IKEA®, but no one ever felt like they've stepped into the showroom," she says. "In fact, people are usually surprised when I tell them, 'That's an IKEA® hack!' I see IKEA® not as the end but the means to an end. It's about self-expression and fun."